PURGATORY LIVING

Stepping out of the purgatory of living
and stepping into a new beginning!

SUMMER BRADSHAU

ISBN-13: 978-0991115907 ISBN-10: 0991115902

DEDICATION

I dedicate this book to everyone who is inspired to step out of the ordinary. Together we can step out of the purgatory of living and step into a new beginning. And to Jessica Salcedo, July 4, 1991 - July 3, 2016- You grew into a beautiful woman and great mother, you stepped out of purgatory living and into a new beginning through the writing of this book, forever shall you be remembered. #JessicasLifeMattered #Love4Jessica

CONTENTS

ACKNOWLEDGMENTS

Those who desire change will change. We only have control of ourselves so let's use that control to be the change within, that the world so desperately needs. So I acknowledge those who are willing to enhance their humanity as people and move forward with change to help create a healthier and prosperous life. To those who are willing to make "life's" sacrifice.

In Summer's World ...

One day I woke up and realized that I was lost for quite some time. I had got comfortable with how life was treating me. I no longer cared about how I presented myself, although I looked great to everyone else, stuck between life and death, you know Purgatory. The real me had left long ago, and the figure that I saw before me was just a shell that protects me until I could be found again. I had everything a woman could ask for and more yet somehow and someway I forgot about myself and ended up in the purgatory of living.

When I had my epiphany, I discovered some things that I should have seen all along but was too busy allowing life to consume me that I didn't care to pay attention. You know, kids, husband, family, work, friends and oh yeah, then me if I'm not too tired...

One day I found myself on the outside of the milk carton... Lost, hanging in the purgatory of living. It was the shock of my life yet not a shock for everyone else. Most often others can see what's going on in your life even when you cannot (or you think you do).

Don't let that to happen to you or to allow it to continue. You can step out of the purgatory of living and into a new beginning. It could be easier than you think it is. For me.

I have some changing to do, and I can only do the changing for me. I cannot change you or the rest of the world, but we can help each other with the process of changing for the better... TOGETHER! And look who we shall find! (You and me too) Let's begin.. how did I **lose myself?**

1 PURGATORY LIVING

I'm lying here in bed, and my eyes are partly open. I can see its light outside but not sure how early it is. I lay my head firmly on the pillow as I think about my life and what the day will bring. I felt different. It is different. I can't explain it really, it's just not the same.

I woke up feeling as if something was not right in my life and that I needed a change. How does one just wake up and the world has changed while they were sleeping?

I no longer wanted to be married, I no longer wanted to wear a size sixteen, and I no longer wanted to be responsible for anyone else but myself.

Wow... That's a lot in one night. I'm really tired and can use a nap. Wait...I don't take naps. So what's really going on?

Life is...different. Like when Adam and Eve were able to tell the difference between right and wrong. They were able to see for the first time that they were naked, as we are now able to see. I can surely see that I am extremely overweight and unhappy. Where have I been in my own life? Living for the need of others and not myself? While surely I love myself, I have always lived, for the need of someone else like my children, husband, friends or relatives.

I woke up one day and wondered why someone didn't tell me I was in autopilot mode. *Good Lord! Look at the mess that is going on.* I am unhappy, overweight, angry, bitter, etc.... Why? What happened that made me lose myself in my own life? How did I end up in the purgatory of living?

My analogy is, you can get caught up in a life that you thought was supposed to happen.

A life you wanted to have, but you didn't know how to live. Sure, some men and women want to give up the bachelor life, but do they even know how to live any other way? How do you (while being in the circle) see what or who is in the circle with you? I think it does take someone else, like a life coach or a therapist to help you to see yourself and your life from the outside looking in.

I woke up and didn't know who I was anymore. I was snappy with everyone like I was in a coma for years and heard them say really bad things or something and now I'm making up for lost time. Well,…they started it…lol!
So you rewind the view master slide and see what has been going on these past years in your life that made you get lost in translation. I mean, someone has got to show you. So here we go…

In Summer's World…

I ended a nine-year relationship with the love of my life because he was not ready to commit, now that says something for a commitment right there, but who's counting? You got a fellow who did not want to be in a relationship to have you as his sidekick for nine whole years, and you felt that marriage should take place. Well yeah! Sometimes people stay in longer relations not being married. Not encouraged for all sorts of legal and moral issues but if it's working, why would you take a hammer to it? Moving on…

Then I meet a guy who would never be my type of guy if I were to choose. But I like his style and his swagger. He is pretty sleek and very business savvy. This gentleman treats you like the queen that you deserve to be treated as. He swoops you up and makes you his Queen. But in real life, things happen, and you start living in defense mode. You move forward as best as you know how but in the process you are drowning in your own vomit because you are trying hard to make the family work but nobody seems to be home.

You no longer care about what you wear, or what you look like because no one is going to see you. You start just being there and not really putting anything into it. You are not kissing anyone, so there is no need to buy lipgloss anymore. You most definitely do not need a nighty. *Hello…pull out the sweats and t-shirts for a comfortable me!* What do you do if you're married and your spouse is never home?
What does your spouse expect you to do, the dishes?
Umm….I don't think so.
I don't know why we fall into that "I'm married now so forget it"

3

mode... not caring what we look like, not caring how we feel and not wanting to make love anymore. One day you are happy and free, and one day you may wake up and go "what the hell is going on here" and "who the heck is in control?"

Things do not always have to remain the same. They may be different and may be out of control now, but you can change anything you want to change tomorrow. We don't have to allow it to control us. We can choose to make a difference. We can choose to allow change to take place, to create the happiness we need in our lives.

We only have control of ourselves, and we can use that control to make a change.

Being married; He's living separately by chance, so I create a life for myself as if I lived alone. I go to the movies alone, out for ice cream alone. I go to dinner alone and oh I go to church alone. Well, now that we determined that I am married, let's see how I lost myself. Really...

The Lost and Found ...

The lost and found is full of people like you and I. Do you think you are the only one that has lost yourself in life? I don't think so. You see...the world is full of lost people and people hanging in the purgatory of living. The list goes on forever, and some of those names on that list would make you surprised. So many movie stars, singers and everyday people you know. You would not think that someone with money could be lost in life, but what you don't know is that often time's, money is the reason for all ills.

Being lost can have something to do with not having the money or having too much money. Not enough money can cause you to lose your house, your family, and your self-respect. Having too much money can cause you to give away too much money, spending on unnecessary things, creating bigger bills and consuming so-called friends who eat you alive.

Losing yourself can have nothing to do with nothing, and you still end up lost just because it's your season to need a reason to redesign your life. Life can be peachy, yet something comes along that makes you think it differently, and you're like, "Whoa! What is this all about?" Just know that when or if that does happen that it's your time to enhance your life somehow. It's not always our time but be ready when it is. And for goodness sakes, be happy for others around you that can enhance their lives even though you cannot at this time.

You can even help out. What a friend you would be!

The Lost and Found; insult to injury,   discovering you were lost and when you were found you were not lost after all. You just needed to make a few minor adjustments and your life transformed into the almost perfect life overnight, your life the way you want it to be lived. Remember, we are living our lives and not other people's lives. They may have some things that you want but do you know in reality consuming your life and space with things, are considered space and money stealers. Be light with your desires, and you will acquire enough to retire.

Sometimes we are not lost and sometimes being found is simply a need to be loved and maybe even hugged. Try becoming friends with someone or rekindling an old friendship. Do things that you normally don't do with others or alone. You are not trapped, you are in transition.

Find some time to figure out what you want and just try some things. If it doesn't work out, well don't do it again, but at least you tried. There will never be a perfect solution to living life, but we can surely make the best of what we have and who we are.

When I found myself, I demanded that everyone else find me as well. That meant that I wanted to be respected for the changes that I chose to make regardless of how anyone felt about it and I didn't care how they felt anyway. It is my life, and I have to live it so there! Ok so... we know that's not the correct way to go about change but it happened, and I'm sorry for it but it is what it is and why must one always sugar coat things? The sooner we can find oneself the better we all will be so help me out here and stop judging and start helping is the message we want to get across.

You may not be the one that needs to be found, but you can help someone who does. We all have a role in this here life, and we are always supposed to help our fellow man or woman whether you know them or not. I want to always be a student in life for a student is always learning something new. Once you learn something, you then teach something and thus the circle of life.

Showing someone how to wear their scarf by not telling them, but by buying one you think would enhance them, and showing them how to style it. Telling someone is a little more offending than actually showing someone unless it's a large ticket item then ok but be nice about how you introduce the subject. We don't want to offend anyone in this new revelation.

Perhaps you are asked, "Excuse me Mr. or Mrs., I found this in the lost and found. Is this yours?" And you reply with an attitude, "Well of course it is! Who else would it be?"

We can only be responsible for ourselves and no one else, so we need to act accordingly.

We should be fulfilling our own fantasies and dreams, life expectancy is what we create it to be. Are we expecting too much from the family and people in our circles or are we only worrying about us and how we are living?

Unless someone else's life, like our children or senior parents, is penetrating our daily activity we need to stay focused. Losing yourself can be detrimental to your health, and if you are not careful, you may not be able to make a comeback. You may just die right there on the sofa or in bed. Have you ever wondered why you lost yourself?

Well, we have no time to think about yesterday, we only can hope to have a tomorrow and when that tomorrow does arrive, we need to be prepared to live it … living it as we are supposed to be living. While we know we live in an imperfect world we must do our part to find a silver lining in the mere fact of waking up each morning.

Finding yourself can be easier than you think. Start small changing one thing at a time. You can purchase a different style shoe than you normally do or try a new haircut. You can find yourself if you simply believe in yourself. No one should have to validate who you are. No one should have to tell you that you are handsome or beautiful. No one should have to tell you that you are doing a great job at being a single parent or helping out your parents.

You should already know you are by your self-satisfaction. Now that you are changing, a piece of who you are should make people want to talk about you. Think about it; if they didn't talk, then you have not done a good job at finding or reinventing yourself. Good change always brings talk of any kind.

The most important thing is the feeling you will get for yourself once you have made some changes. It is not important what others think, as long as you are happy. Everyone has their version of how we are supposed to be, and that may not be how we want to be. If we are not judging others, then others may not need to judge us. In the end, we will not concern ourselves with the foolish things people do or say; we will only be concerned with being happy today.

Remembering to ...

Remember that you are to make small changes. One at a time or a few at a time ... whatever you can do comfortably.

- Smile more

- Listen to music

- Buy new shoes

- Compliment someone

- Buy new underwear

- Change your hairstyle

- Buy new lipstick

- Buy new cologne or scented lotions

Anything that you do that is different from before is considered a change. If it enhances your life and does not make you look bad or represent you falsely, we are open to positive change. Anyone can make changes. You have to want to change for it to stay in effect. Your desire will allow the positive energy to flow where it needs to flow thus creating a happier and healthier being. Your body will love you, for it will now be able to grow as intended and heal as needed. Being happy is your choice and every day brings a new chance for new change.

Things that you do in your everyday life will enable you to bring as much happiness as you would like it. When you decide to change something from the normal, positive things will always occur whether you realize it or not.

HAIRCUT

New Attitude

New Pep In
Your Step

NEW CLOTHING

Smile More

Create
Conversation

Just taking small, simple steps is all you need! Remember you don't have to spend a lot or nothing at all if you know someone who can give you a new haircut or clothing. Anything helps.

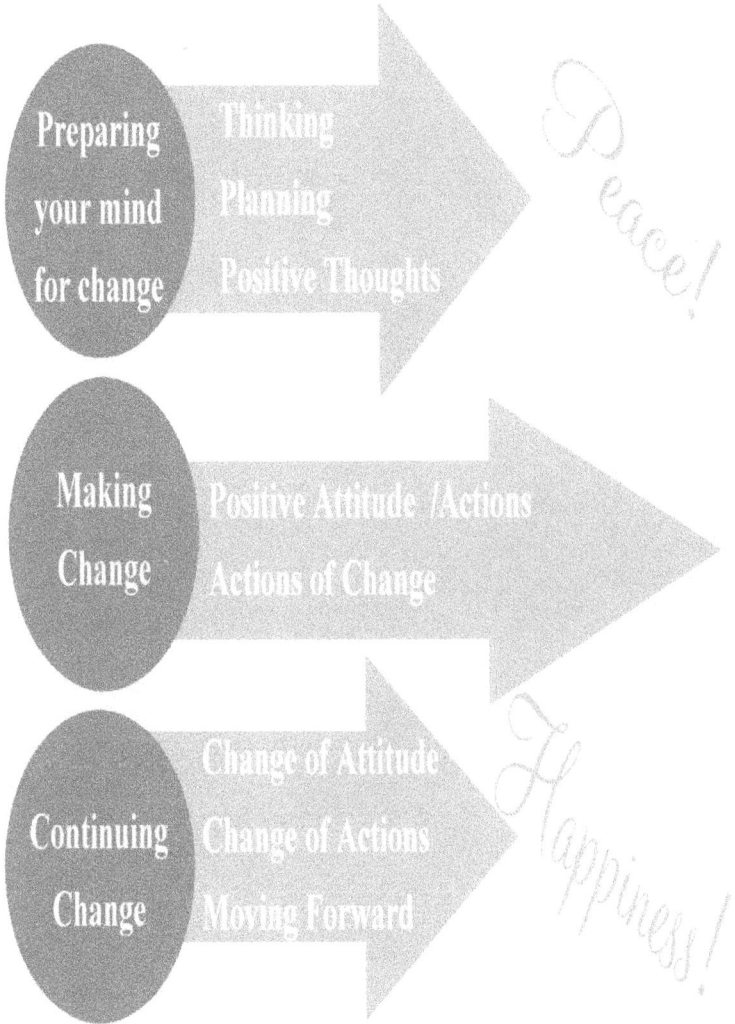

NOTES:

2 Married or Not. Here you come

Wherever you are ... there you will always be. You can never run from yourself or your problems, so let's learn to live with who we are, today. Maybe you're married or may wish to be one day. You have a spouse/friend that you love and have created this great life for. Now it's time for children and the American dream. Working in the world and taking care of home and family. An experience of a lifetime...

But what happens is you grow in auto pilot mode. Everything's the same and nothing exciting happens. Life, my friends, is what you make it. Just because you're married does not mean you cannot have a fun, loving life. You can take the kids to the sitters and go out and dance. Eat dinner on the terrace or make love in the car, when was the last time you made out in the backseat of your car? And, how fun was that? If not, oh my God, you have to try it!

Being married/dating should be fun and exciting. The anticipation of the one you love walking in the front door. The feeling in your stomach that makes your heart sing when you're pulling into the driveway, the throb that takes you by surprise when you look into their eyes as if for the first time. Life does not have to be depressing phone calls and drama to name a few. Pulling into the driveway dreading going inside while you sit there acting like you need to make a call first; you even go as far as cleaning out the car so you don't have to go in, you're home if they call or look out of the window, but you're not at home, yelling "Go inside and wait till I get there!" When the hubby asks, "What's for dinner?" Do you get angry and go off?

We do not have to create drama; it's all unnecessary. Being married/dating is communicating and respecting. We can acknowledge the other, and know…no one is perfect. You should be able to dress up and go out, hit a movie and hot dog stand. Take the kids out to the beach or fun zone. Hanging out in the library can even be fun. You have to create happiness for your self in your own life. No one is responsible for your happiness. So what are you doing to make yourself happy?

In Summer's World …

So I'm chilling in the marriage and not caring about anything. The hubby does his thing, and I do mine. Nowhere really are we meeting in the middle. We don't even say goodnight to each other, now that's bad, and if you mention sex.

We are different in the way we think, so, that's natural. He does not like the way I think… I think that if no one is dying or bleeding to death, then it's not that important, things can be a lot worse. He feels he wants to handle everything and everything is an issue. Well, my life is too short for that. I can care less...

So went the marriage, he lived it alone, and I did as well. That's how marriages end but in the process ... I have lost myself... in life and marriage. Marriage I know is giving and take, and we both did most of what is called of us, but what happens when those two people grow in different directions and the other isn't very pleased or doesn't want to go in that direction? Or say, for instance, my ex-husband felt I should listen to him more, and I felt he should value my opinion and respect the fact that his wife is real and does exist. Every marriage will have its issues. It's how you approach and handle the issues that are the main focus.

Not willing to change and try something different will cause you great depression and thus you can get lost in someone else's misery or life. Evaluate what is going on in your marriage or relationship and see what you can do to change it without coming across as controlling.

You have to be the better person, and you have to be willing to change yourself. If you have not been wearing makeup or getting a haircut at the barber's, do so. Make the change and sacrifice if it is required to make a difference. You will feel better about yourself on the inside as well as the outside. People will smile because you are smiling, adds a little bounce to your step, man or woman. Go out and buy a new dress, you don't have to get an expensive one but get something new for yourself, put a little pep in your step. New hair and makeup is essential, even if it's just a trim and how about a new tie?

Watch how your spouse or significant other notices your step. It's different if you're not changing together. But if you are in love…why not change together? There is something about everyone that can use a little change. Try to make it fun and exciting.

I've met several couples, like **Sandy and Doug**, an awesome couple who have been married for over 25 years and they still love each other like it's for the first time. I love watching them grow in their relationship; for I can see their love and smile is very genuine. They have that "when we first met" glare for each other that is simply amazing. I want what they have yet I have to understand that love like that is now rare but always possible if two people want it to be.

Even if you're not married, changes are essential. Being single can be just as fun as getting together with friends or alone. I enjoy getting out alone at times and meeting up with friends a few times a month. It's good for you to know and learn more about yourself at this time, so spending some time alone can create a great balance in your new life.

Looking in my view master, I see that I was forced into lonesome journeys(not on purpose). The ex-husband was always away at work or with friends in his spare time. There was not much "us" time. It was "he" or it was "I" but hardly a "we."

Being married can bring us sometimes to wonder. *What is my worth? What is my value to this marriage? Who am I really because I seem to take care of everyone else and not myself? Well, what about me?* Huh, really, what about me? Single people actually can experience this as well.

Even if you are content, as you may think, and seem to have a happy life with your significant other and family, there is always room to make yourself a little happier. Nothing's wrong with adding a little more fun to the plate.

The plate can never be too full of fun. Just imagine the different aspects of the relationship you can bring to the table: outdoor fun, indoor fun, and bedroom fun. Just make a list of things and throw them in a hat and *presto!* See where you go from there. You can do things without spending any money at all. Both of you should agree on what you want and work to make it happen. Now, how much fun that can be? You must both agree that change can be fun and be willing to make it happen.

13

Being Single ...

Being single feels lonely at times, but if you were with someone, maybe you would be tired of them and wishing you were single again. If you are single, take advantage of the free time to love yourself. Treat yourself special, take yourself out to dinner, and/or buy yourself something nice. Being single should be a time when you learn how to do you. If you are not happy, no one in your circle will be happy.

While you are single, you can sample different things. You can date someone with a different nationality than yourself (if you're into that) or date someone with a different career than yours. Figure out what kind of man or woman will make you happy before one comes your way. If it's not the man or woman of your dreams, then let him or her keep going. The goal is for you to be happy in your life. Others cannot determine your happiness, but they sure can add to it. Be careful with whom you choose friendship.

If you want to see the world, whether you're married or not, please find a way to make it happen. We have to live to be happy, not tomorrow, but today. Oh, how nice it would be for me to live in Paris. I would like to make that happen. I can see myself writing in Paris, sitting on my terrace and sipping tea. Where would you like to be?

We don't have to have a million dollars to do something that makes us happy. Being wise with our decisions and our willingness to sacrifice, working harder and being what we need to be for this to take place. Pushing forward with whatever it is in life that you want and need. It won't happen while you're sitting there hiding behind your newspaper in curlers and a cigarette hanging out of your mouth. Or how many soccer games do you have to attend before you are an official advocate for space stealing?

Myspace is being stolen from me against my will ... Children can take up a lot of your time, so it's wise to plan ahead when it comes to their sports and activities. It may not be a good time for one of your children to be in baseball right now because daddy would not have any time to breathe if he had to attend all practice and regularly scheduled games. If daddy has no time to breathe, mommy will not be happy, and then the child will not be happy as well. The whole house is now in disarray and marriage is falling apart just because you insisted on William playing baseball this season.

It was unnecessary. Also, mom may not want to spend her every free hour toting children to ballet and softball practice after work and still trying to be a wife and friend and daughter and niece and aunt and all the other things people are expecting of her. I am willing to sacrifice some of my life, but I need some for myself. I mean if you don't take any time for you, then what do you think ends up happening to you? You end up in a bad relationship or parentship, and you don't understand how you got there. You end up in the purgatory of living.

I know children can be so much fun, and you would not change a thing about them. But sometimes change is needed for the adults to be able to have a peace of mind and some me time.

Making time for you, whether you're married or not is important. I know single people who thought they were taking care of themselves and once we mapped it out, they saw differently. It's amazing how when you get someone else to analyze your life, you see how what you were thinking, was nowhere near the truth. If you can handle it, get someone to do just that, analyze your life.

Once you have determined that you do have some issues that may need working out, you can feel comfortable enough to go ahead and start making changes. How good you will feel once you have talked it out in your mind. It's a whole mind game that you have to play with yourself and everyone else. That's all life is. Play your game right, and you can always be the winner.

Remember to take time for yourself...

Would your family have a problem with you enrolling in a class or two? If not, then take a class at a local college or adult school. You can even take a dance or yoga class.

Go to the gym and library. Do just about anything that will enhance you and get you out of the house catering to yourself and not others.

You have to take the time for you. Your husband or wife may or may not like the new you. If you jumped right into changing your life... he or she may not be able to handle it all; especially if you were in purgatory as the lonely looking housewife or husband. You see, now you have to have permission to leave the house. So be careful how you jump into sexy. The world is not always ready for you.

You may have to ease into things a little bit. Don't put everyone in a coma right away. Change comes with time and you can't or should not rush it. But if you feel you need to leave the house before something bad happens, by all means, rush; otherwise, you can ease into the new you if you choose to. Male or female, single or married, you will impact the world on who you will become.

Being who you want to be and choose to can be the best thing in the world. You have all the choices in life to create it how you see fit. Alone or married, you have a right to want to listen to music, you have a right to want to go to a drive-in movie, alone or with a friend and it doesn't always have to be with your loved one. Everyone should have some me time, and by all means, this can include people other than your spouse or friends. When we want to create happiness for ourselves we chose whom to include and whom not to include. We can go where we would like to go versus always having to go where others want to go. Think about how you want your life to be lived and start living it.

Wherever you go … there you shall be, always. You can never run from yourself, but you can surely make others run from you. Be careful how you eliminate the unnecessary people and things in your life.

We often blame others for our failure or our resentments, but if you pull out the view master slide (looking at the past of failures and heartaches), again we will see that you had some choices in the matters, but you made the wrong choices which created an unwanted outcome. Often others are never to blame for our unhappiness. We allow others to say and do things in our life, we allow others to have control over our lives, and as you know, people only do to you what you allow them to do to you. So how much are you allowing and what happened to your control?

If you are single, you have way more control over your life than those that are married. Single people can come and go as they please without having to check in with a spouse or they can travel without the need to drag someone along that didn't want to go in the first place. There are always advantages to being single. Think of all the drama that you are missing out on by being in control of your own life. If you are not living with anyone and you make your own money, well, what's your problem? Who has your butt tied in a wad?

Single people are actually hated by married people because they have more freedom. They can date whomever they wish to date, stay home when they want, eat out when they want, and please let's not mention the fact that someone is not constantly asking you for the remote. Enjoy being single for single always has an advantage. The disadvantages can be huge, but for the most part, lonely comes when you are with someone as well so…. How are you living? And are you happy with it?

I remember being more lonely when I was married than I was when I was single. Being single allowed me more outside time and friend times. Being married has limits and often can cut those times out altogether, intentional or not.

Wanting to start a new life begins with wanting a new you. There are unlimited amounts of possibilities, life is **LIMITLESS**.

You can be anything you choose to be, and I choose to be happy regardless of what is going on around me. How can I create that for myself and others without sacrificing all of me?

◆◆◆◆◆◆◆◆◆◆◆◆◆◆

RECIPE FOR HAPPINESS

1.5 hours of "you time" per day

1 cup of appreciation for yourself

1oz of courage to want to and implement your happiness

1 can of whoop ass … never allow others to steal your joy

◆◆◆◆◆◆◆◆◆◆◆◆◆◆

Taking time for you, to go to the movies, beach, dinner or get a new hairdo or haircut is essential in creating happiness for yourself. Keep an open mind as all may not go according to plan you may have to alternate or reschedule.

Always know that you deserve to have time for yourself. Appreciate you for who and what you are today and never allow anyone to interfere or talk you out of taking care of you.

There are always people who will want to steal your joy but don't allow them to. Put your foot down and demand the respect you deserve. Courage to take care of yourself without the expectation of someone else to do it for you is huge. We often don't do what we want to do in life because we are afraid to take that chance, to make that jump that we need to make. Know that you can do all things that you want to do if you first want to do it!

When you create your recipe for love, make sure that it is something that is realistic enough actually to take place. Be as creative as you want to be when planning out your recipe for love.

17

RECIPE FOR LOVE

One night of alone time

Four cups of anticipation

Three oz of kinkiness

Six chocolate covered strawberries with-

One glass of whip cream

One sexy nightgown and silk boxers

Five scented candles

Three cups of rose petals

❖❖❖❖❖❖❖❖❖❖❖❖❖

Text each other about the anticipation of the date, let the other know how excited you are. Be a little graphic and hint a few things you may do to each other. Buy or pull out your most sexy lingerie or underwear.

Look fabulous so you will feel fabulous and add some scented candles to the bedroom or hotel room. It's ok to get a hotel room even if it's in the same town you live to add some spice to your life, away from home, the usual. Pick up some rose petals from your local florist and sprinkle them on dark colored sheets of your own or in the bath that you will take together. Ooh…what a great night this can be if you chose it to be!

❖❖❖❖❖❖❖❖❖❖❖❖❖

RECIPE FOR FUN

4 hours of time

2 tickets to a movie

1 reservation for dinner

1 cup of happiness

1 oz of encouragement

4 spoons of love

10 kisses

You and your loved one can have a date night. See a movie and go out to dinner, without the kids or other couples. Get a couple massage, how fun. Encourage yourself as well as your loved one to make the time and commitment to keeping the date. Positive words should be all you need to create happiness if only for today. Try holding hands, rubbing your fingers on his/her back, winking when you're caught staring.

There are so many ways to have fun and show love for one another. The ultimate fun date is one full of kisses from both parties... Steal them when he/she is not looking and right when a man is staring at your woman, grab her and go for the standing ovation. Once you let her up for air, let's just say you will officially be the man!

You can create any fun you need to create so that you are happy... simple as that. A movie, a comedy show, the beach or whatever you like. We have to create our lives how we want it to be, and happy should always be our number one goal. Once you learn it, you will be able to have it as part of your everyday.

Be something or someone you have always wanted to be that is, for a real reason. Loving yourself will help you to become that person, but make sure to keep it realistic.

#SheBecameAComedian I have a social media friend who is a comedian. Her name is Adele Givens, she is one of the Queens of Comedy and always "such a lady." I simply love watching her life on social media because she keeps herself and her family (the pieces she shares) very real. She one day knew she was funny so she became a comedian, and we fell in love. She doesn't just share jokes (believe it or not everything isn't funny), she shares her real emotions, funny or not. I watched her go through so much when her husband went through a few transplants (it was made public), her sons graduated or had birthdays and more.

She laughs when life gives her jokes, and she cries when things require tears. But most importantly, she's true to herself and those around her. She keeps it very real and, like myself, a good woman can appreciate that. I have watched her through her entire career, but now I can appreciate the laughter much better. I have grown, she has grown, her funny has grown into something great. Doing what you love makes life a little easier.

To be happy, I treated myself to a recent comedy show over at a local venue to see The Queen Of Comedy herself, Ms. Adele. ***To just sit back and laugh and laugh some more*** was the best time of my life and not to mention I got to meet her and hug her and steal some of her positive energy (laughing). She is just as real in person, on stage as she is on social media and I love that about her. She also stated that next time she was in town, we should do lunch. hhhmmm hhhmmm I'm holding you and Tone to that lol. #TheOriginalAdele #WhosAlwaysALady

Treat yourself to some comedy. If you cannot afford to go out then watch some on the internet. Laughing is essential to living.

The Queens of Comedy is very funny, and we are thankful they realized their calling. Some of us have a calling, and we don't realize what it is, or we passed it up. But ... it's never too late to be who you need to be or desire to be. Most famous people started late in life, and so can you.

Choosing comedy to make people laugh, and forget about the everyday strain of life. Teaching us that even though you may have real-life situations, laughter will always help you get through it. Funny is what funny does, and I thank those that have the gift of laughter.

Although everything is not a laughing matter, you can learn so many things if you just sit and be a people watcher. You will always do great when you learn not to react when angry or confused. You have to keep yourself mellow at all times so that all can be well, issue or not. You have control over how you react to the things that go on around you in life. The best way to solve all things is to always keep to yourself. You can even laugh (laughing). Be warned; people don't always like laughter so be cautious as to how funny life is out loud lol. We don't want to awake the laughterslayers.

Quote from Adele Givens, Comedian, regarding purgatory living

I believe we don't get stuck in life. We get caught up in the belief that we're stuck. Life takes us EXACTLY where we are supposed to be at EXACTLY the time we need to be there. In an odd way, feeling stuck is actually your growth. You have no option except to grow. ~Adele Givens

https://www.facebook.com/Adele-Givens-Too

If you learn not to interact when not needed, you can save yourself a lot of stress. You have to allow friends and family to fight their battle without you sometimes. You have to keep that happiness in your life, and the best way to do that is to keep your own business.

If you offer opinions to people, they will tell someone else, and then you are a part of a circle of gossip, and you could have avoided all of that by keeping your own business. Allow other people to work out their own life without you adding yourself even if asked.

Learn to say no in a way that is not offending but firm enough it gets the point across.

You are trying to create a new life and a new happiness, and you teach people how to treat you first by how you treat yourself. Learn how to use the control that you have over you.

You can only control how you react or act so please react accordingly. You have to be aware that people will always try to steal your joy but you cannot allow that to happen. Just stick to what you know and be well with it.

Every day that you open your eyes is a new learning experience. You can have a pleasant experience or a bad one; it's your choice. One more step out of Purgatory Living and one more step into your new beginning. There goes that control again. You only can do what you have the power to do, and you do have the power to be happy and make everyone around you happy as well. The more you learn on this journey, the more you teach along the way.

It's a way of saying thanks for the upgrade. You have to share that knowledge with others so that they too can live a happy life. Life is always a learning experience, and one must always be a student.

The ability to learn is a gift. Once you receive the gift, you must pay forward the gift by teaching. To not teach after receiving the gift of learning, would be stealing knowledge. And we, my friends, are no thieves; so please teach everyone you can, the things that life brings.

Schedule yourself on your calendar so that you have enough time for yourself, something that is very important to your happiness and growth.

EXAMPLE:

SCHEDULE	
9:00am	Work
10:00am	Meeting
11:30am	Lunch
2:00pm	Work
3:45pm	Bank
4:30pm	Mani/Pedi ME time ☺
5:45pm	Dinner at The Bradshau Hotel
7:00pm	Hot tub
8:00pm	Dessert/Wine
9:00pm	Movie in bed

Remembering to ...

Remember to create a list of things that you can do, alone or with someone. Learn to have fun alone, so you are not sitting at home sulking in life. Remember to watch some comedy and just laugh. Laughing is essential to living.

- Movies/Comedy/Funny
- Laugh
- Dinner
- Flea Market
- Book Store
- Fashion Show
- Get a Massage, together or single
- Visit the Park for a walk or a book
- Coffee or Tea shop, sit, and people watch

It helps to get out there and do some things. It helps to keep you motivated and allows you to see new things. You don't have to over-do it, just a little at a time.

NOTES: Don't feel so hammered out of life. Make some immediate changes.

Mario Sanchez

3 Losing Yourself – Literally

How does one lose their self in life … literally? Take a look in the mirror, then pull out the view master and see for yourself (the past 15 years of your life). Only you know where you have been all these years.

I can see from the looks of people in the world that a great majority have lost themselves in life. And sometimes it has nothing to do with marriage or relationships. Sometimes we just lose our self in life and don't even know we are lost.

How many people do you see that go to work, come home and don't have the time or energy to do anything else? They watch television, drink beer or sleep until it's time to do it again. And the cycle repeats itself every day of every week. The weekends are no different. Some people complain about not having enough time to do anything. Some people sleep most of the weekend, eat out, and complain that they don't have energy.

Ok, view master, please. Come on…look at the slide. Clearly you can see when you live your life in that cycle; you are in robot mode. You're doing the same things over and over again without any change. You're pulling yourself into what looks like a washing machine, and you're going round and round but you can't seem to pull yourself out, and you just keep going in circles. ♫♪ *You got me going in circles* … ♫♪

Ok, seriously, that is no way to live your life. You are supposed to be able to enjoy the fruits of your labor. How else do you live? You were not born a robot, and you were certainly not supposed to be one now.

You have to make time for you so that happiness is present in your life at all times. You cannot make it in life just working and not adding any flavor. If I served you a boiled chicken and did not season it, would you like it? That would not sit well with you.

So when you live in a robot stage, you are depriving yourself of spice, fun, and adventure. Why do you think you have weekends off? (Hopefully, or at least some time off.) Now if you want to sleep in, fine... go right ahead and sleep in, but at some point, you need to get out and go to the store ... ice cream or a movie, something that would take you out for a moment of fresh air and hear voices of others.

For those of us who live alone, you have to know that getting out and being around other grownups is good for you. If you are not around grown-ups regularly, join a club or group where you can interact with people.

Losing yourself can happen in so many ways if you allow it to. Getting married and taking care of the needs of your spouse. Taking on a job where the demand of you is so high that you don't even have time for yourself. Having children and all your time and energy goes into them. Losing yourself by no longer looking in the mirror and caring what you look like on the outside. You may feel beautiful on the inside, but if you don't look decent, your inner beauty will suffer as well.

You can begin collecting something and get carried away with the collection itself. Next thing you know, it's affecting the way you interact with your family and eventually how you feel about yourself. You have officially lost yourself in life and marriage. But you can get it back. Start by eliminating something that is bringing you down, even if that something is a person. Anyone or anything that is interfering with your life should be evaluated and determined if it should be removed and deemed unnecessary or if it should be kept.

There are so many ways that someone can lose themselves. Sometimes we take on more of life than we were supposed to. This can create time loss and puts a strain on family life. You get caught up in the fights and promises. No one wants to limber in Purgatory, but if you are not careful before you know it, you will see yourself hanging there with no way out.

Pay close attention to how some people dress. Look at the clothing pattern of some people, notice how they stop dressing nicely or they just have a plain dress on them like they don't put thought into it.

They have to get dressed, but they don't have to like it. Well, it kind of makes you happy or sad, the way you dress. If you're not putting thought into the way you are presenting yourself to the public, then you are not caring how you feel about yourself as well. And your family may not like it.

Some people say it does not matter how they look. But the reality is that your subconscious mind reacts to how people react to you. And you know when people are questioning your clothing decisions, you will react in a defense mode. Some people will even stop seeing friends because their friends don't care for the way they dress. When you don't want to hear someone's mouth, you stop going around them. #Truth

Losing yourself in Purgatory can be a really bad thing. For some people, it's more than your attire. It's the way you cut off friends. The way you eat more to make you happy. You don't go out much. You allow people to make you bitter; You are always angry. You can be going through a divorce, need a job, don't have money and the rest of what life brings as we all will go through things in life, it's how we go through it that determines our outcome. Know what is making you feel lost and make some changes for yourself, or if you know someone else that has been in purgatory living, share from experience. Everyone should have a testimony and testimonies are not to be kept to oneself.

As for myself, I woke up realizing that I had been lost in Purgatory for years. I could not figure out who I was. Purgatory living is what I was doing.
What happens that makes you see the light? What happens that makes you wake up one day, and your life is different? You can now see everything for what it is. ♫♪ "I can see clearly now the rain is gone... I can see all obstacles in my way!" ♫♪

And the unfortunate part is that you can't keep it to yourself. You start acting out on people, the family like they are supposed to know that you woke up different. You have been allowing the whole world to piss on you, per say, and now you have woken up, and you want to say something about it. What the hell is wrong with you? Are you PMSing, going through menopause, life crises or something? (This is what my family was thinking.)

Everyone is looking at you strangely and wondering why you are tripping. You don't even know why you're tripping, but you have to keep up this charade because this is how you feel even if you don't know why.

Well now ... tripping or not, you need to get it together. To be honest, as I always am... it is unnecessary to be going off on everyone because you changed. You have to pull it together and get the results you want with less of a roar. Just because you lost yourself, you better check yourself before you wreck the entire household ... happens all the time.

Losing yourself in Purgatory is easy to do, but when you're ready ... you can make a comeback. Guarantee it ... But your mind has to be receptive, willing to make the necessary changes that are required of you.

Like, how about taking lunch instead of eating out every day ... or how about cooking dinner for two days in a row instead one ... gets a heads up on the week.

Losing yourself will happen before you can say I do. Is it extra weight? You only are with children every day ... all day? You see more of your husband's ass than you do your own?

If you picked up this book, then you know that you are lost. Somehow someway... and yes there is hope. If you were to stare into a mirror, what would you see? Who would you see? In that mirror, who would you be? How lost are you?

Losing yourself, for the most part, is hard to admit because you are on the inside and cannot see what is going on. Everyone else of whom does not reside with you can tell you how lost you are... people can see it, you cannot! Or maybe don't want to admit it. Either way... you're lost.

We can decide what and whom we want to be and be it ... anytime we choose to. The keyword here is Choose. Choose to be happy, choose to have a great day regardless of the circumstance, and choose to have peace.

Once you have decided that you want to be happy or happier ... you can, it's a mind thing. Make up your mind right now, today ... I want to be happy, I want to change, and I want to be different.

I'm sure you are fine just the way you are, but everyone can use some fine-tuning. Getting a refresher course or what not is ok. When you wake up in the morning, you can be different … if you want to.

You can make small changes that won't even appear to change at all. Ask your friends how they see you can make a difference. It may be fun to include your family and friends once you decide you want to make that change. They can see what the real you are like. They have talked about it already behind your back; use that to your advantage.
Take control of the only thing in life that we have control over … ourselves.

You can make it fun … it doesn't have to be a task.   We   are making life so complex that there are way too many things, people and stuff. You get caught up in stuff and yeah … you can lose yourself.

So we can evaluate our stuff and see what's unnecessary. Once we have determined the unnecessary, we can start eliminating. Eliminating things that are no longer working for you… you know all those trips to the hair shop only to be sweated out by Reggie over on Crenshaw.

You might as well do your hair and save that money. Saving that money allows a little financial freedom for the moment.
Once you start learning new ways to do new things, you can pull yourself out of being lost.

The Unnecessary …

The unnecessary thing about being, wasted thoughts that use energy to feed itself into an obese space, taking time away from things of importance and things of need. To oneself, the unnecessary is like forsaking the potential of what is to come. Breathing it in like the pillow that floats above made of toxic waste. The unnecessary thought, time, duty, privilege, desire, need, or just about any unnecessary thing in life, is like dying right after you win the lotto.

Filling us with bad fatty acid in the make-believe world of consumption, consummating how many years do we actually lose doing and feeling unnecessary things. Free your mind and your spirit by doing things that are pleasing and beneficial to your soul. Thinking of days of new with you in mind ready and willing to change the course to a new and beautiful direction, just over the horizon is what you have been waiting for all of your

29

life.

The unnecessary things in life are cradle robbers and grim reapers. They steal the space that is needed in your soul that requires you to nurture and love it to all of the eternity. The one thing that is required of you in this lifetime is an alliance to yourself.

The unnecessary things in life require half of your time and energy. Imagine how much time you can gain in life by deleting the unnecessary.

The friend that takes too much of your time and space, you have to ask yourself, do I need this person in my life? Is the friendship necessary? Is the cleanup of the friendship too much?

The unnecessary stuff in life is consuming too much of you and if you do not delete it, it will eat you like the acid that drips from your car battery.

The unnecessary is just that, Unnecessary, not needed to be exact. You didn't' have to say it or do it. You especially didn't have to listen to it or try to explain it. It was simply unnecessary in the first place. You do not need to know what Kim's friend's name is. Unless you need to conduct business with or will be seeing on a regular, stop asking unnecessary questions or expect people to tell you every unnecessary thing in life. It's way too unnecessary.

Think about some of the fights you have had in your lifetime, unnecessary. You should not have to go through stuff like that. Deal with the situation and keep it moving. How about the arguments, well, aren't we grown up enough to be able to talk to each other about it without getting that angry?

I mean we are all different, and yelling is totally unnecessary. No one is going to think like the other. Know your differences and keep it moving.

Unnecessary spending, well now ladies, don't say a word. It's not what you buy most often; it's why you buy it. Men and their cars ...well how many do you really need? If you make a list of everything you have purchased this year, you will find that more than half was an unnecessary purchase and if you total the amount of money each item cost you, you will see how much money you have wasted. It was all unnecessary.

Unnecessary work habits will do you the same. Put in your two hundred percents so that when you slack up, you are still over the top. It's not necessary to always take credit for everything you do. Show up for work late, why? Why do you need to be late to work other than real appointments, because you're lazy? Unnecessary behavior…

Free the space in your mind so that your transition into your golden years will be one full of necessary memories of times of old and new. Not just a blank stare …

It's up to you to control your HAPPINESS! Anything else is UN-NECESSARY!

Now, let's start by making a list, yeah …the list, the list of things in your life that you do on a daily basis and the reasons why you do them.

Here is the list of my life:

LIST OF THINGS I DO DAILY

Activity	Necessary	Delegate
Pack Lunches	Yes	Yes
Drop Kids off	Yes	2 days
Drive to work	Yes	No
Stop at store	No	Prepare on time off
Pick Up Kids	No	Can catch the bus
Drop kids at- Practice	Yes	No
Cook Dinner	Yes	Yes

Create your list as you need it to be as long as you create it. As you can see, there are some things that you may do every day, but when you write it down and look it in detail and why you may do it, you can see that you can eliminate or re-delegate some things. By doing that you create some you time that you most desperately need to survive.

However, you see you need to make the changes necessary to do so. Everyone may not be happy about the new arrangements, but if you can explain in detail why the changes are necessary, everyone should be on the same team. The family is working together for the good of surviving if only for one day.

Some things may be weekly or monthly. So you can make three columns if you like. But let's just keep it simple and get the list done.

On that list... which items are unnecessary? Maybe they can be given to someone else to do. Can you delegate that task? If so, circle it and put the name of the person by it so you can see if it's possible to pass over. You have to get yourself out of where you are so it's important to eliminate things in your life.

So now you have accomplished a lot if you were able to eliminate anything on your list or delegate to. Give yourself high five for that one.

If you keep that process for everything you do in life ... trust me when I say, you will eliminate a lot of unnecessary in your future faster than you did in your past. You're Upgraded!

Remembering to ...

- Remove the unnecessary things in your life.
- Make a list of what you do in your everyday life and see if it can be eliminated or delegated to someone else.
- Understand you only have control over you and you only have a limited amount of awake time to be all that you can be.
- Free your mind of things that do not concern you.
- Eliminate people using you.
- Disable the YES button from your vocabulary.
- Make sure to do things that are pleasing to you.
- Don't be a robot in your life ... hit the reset button.
- Find out who you are and what you like and go for it.
- Don't worry about what others think of you ... loving yourself will always take care of that.
- Live for who you are today ... not yesterday or tomorrow
- Review your view master slides; you're not where you were; not where you might be, but have a great opportunity to be who you need to be!

(song I found reminds me of purgatory living, for real. R rated)

GREEDY GEEZ x HOT BOI JUICE - HEAVEN OR HELL
https://youtu.be/_WVT_7wBH5Q

NOTES:

4 Upgrade Me Please!

Now that you know you can use a little upgrading... now what? Now, what do you do to change your life? If you don't know, find someone who can help you. If you think you can figure it out, take your time and write it out, that will help you remember things in your life that you may be in need of changing. You can always contact me, and we can go through it together.

Upgrading yourself from whom and what you are now is easier than it sounds. It's little things that add up to bigger things that appear to swallow us whole from the feet up.

We are in such a stage of denial we believe our own stories about why we are sixty pounds overweight ... I got health issues; my thyroid is acting up. How about just rearranging the foods you eat to match the breakdown system of things. Or you can eliminate some stuff on the menu altogether. Pay attention to the time you eat certain items or meals; it really makes a difference in weight gain and/or attitude.

For you to be upgraded, you have to change some stuff. Everyone can't always handle change, but you can do it when your mind is ready to change your body will follow. Care about what and how you eat. Care about the way you present yourself inside and out. You now have to work a little bit harder on yourself. So yeah ... you may not like this new revolution because of all the hard work or you may just freaking love it!

Upgrade me, please! That's all I keep hearing in my ears. Upgrade me ... that simple. My mind is made up... and it is receptive to change. I am willing to do what is necessary by first eliminating the unnecessary.

I can do all things with my power and will.

I am officially... UPGRADED! Now, how simple is that? You have to start making those changes. Today!

When you visit the grocer, make sure to get fresh fruits and vegetables and the rest of whatever it is you like. You only need to make small changes in your diet.

Try eliminating fast food. Most fat comes from fast food eating, if you need it, maybe once a week. You have to work at making lunch or going to a more expensive restaurant-style eating (that can be more costly).

I teach people to take a cooler in your vehicle or office so that you can have fruit and vegetables and lunch available when you need it. It's a perfect solution to a healthier lifestyle.

Makes a huge difference in your weight once you start paying attention to the intake of bad foods. It becomes easier as you move on to eating better and healthier.

Don't put too much stress on yourself about things. It should not be stressful to upgrade yourself. It may be an adjustment but never stressful. If it's stressful, back off it for a while and reevaluates.

Try to eat your dinner before seven o'clock. The world says six in the evening, but these days, you have to be realistic. So to make it easier for me to accomplish, I say seven. And it's easier for me to accomplish... so!

Make it easy for yourself. Upgrade me, please! Upgrading can be so much fun if you allow it to be. I learned how to upgrade myself the hard way, but wow, when I did, it was an awesome feeling.

So, while I was lost, I added some unnecessary weight. That weight was pretty significant for me. I have always been a small frame, but once I got lost in life, I silently gained weight. You know, you wake up one day, and you can't fit any of your clothes, and you are like, what the hell, and you knew last year you were gaining weight and didn't do anything about it. So ... now I lost fifty pounds doing what I love to do... dancing.

I danced into a better me...literally! Now that's a word I can keep. I danced, and I danced, and the music was so loud, and I was so happy. My son William thought I was crazy. He couldn't believe all the music and the fact that every day I was dancing my heart out. I made some people mad, namely Chris and Martin (my play sons) but as you can see, the results paid off significantly, so big ups to Chris and Martin for toleration. Some people are going to have to tolerate some things from you as you go through this transition. Let them know you care but not really (laughing).

I turned on that radio, and I grooved to some really good music. I did not use any routines or DVDs. I danced my dance.

Now that I'm healthier, I'm upgrading. Oh, how nice it feels! I have new clothes, a new attitude, a new reason to live, and new hope for my new life. I'm healthier and wiser in my mind. I'm healthier in my spirit. I'm happier than I have ever been at a time in my life when I should not want to live. Why? I'm UPGRADED! And you have to want to be upgraded to get there.

I have been making the necessary changes in my life to be Upgraded. I have lost weight, and I eat healthier. I live healthier, and I am healthier in a whole. I am happy, I am sad, I am human, yet I live... and that makes it all worth it. And now we have the opportunity to share that with the world. I need you to be Upgraded TODAY!

I see a chiropractor, which helps me feel better. I get my adjustments that help my body and my immune system, and you can do it do. It's for every aspect of your life. Sinus, migraine, posture, immune, etc. Learn what makes your body operate and grow so you can live longer. One of my chiropractors teaches you about your body so that you can better take care of it. Dr. John Gutierrez is a specialist in health and body and knows the spine very well. I'm thankful for the knowledge so that I can self-help my future.

No more excuses for why you can't change. Just do it. You just pick up a cigarette when you want to, or you buy fast food when you desire. You can do what you are willing to do. So... change.

Glad to hear you're ready to change (smile). We can do it together. As you are reading this ... so are so many others that are going through the same things. It's a cycle of life. It's what we do and what we are made of. But right now, you have the opportunity to be upgraded. No more broken down housewives. No more couch potato husbands. Upgrade them. It's time to make that change.

If you can realize that the whole world is going through the same stuff at the same time, we can get through some stuff a little bit easier than not.

You are not alone. You are on your way to being upgraded. So now that you are making some small changes in your life, you want to make sure that your attitude stays correct, happy and carefree yet at the same time, always respectful. The rest of the world should be able to see that you are changing without having to participate in the cycle.

It can affect some of your close relatives, especially if they have never seen you in your new you. So be aware of their feelings. While you have a right to do you, you still have to be at least considerate.

Upgrading is noticeable by all. So always be respectful and lady or man-like. And by all means, have fun doing it too. You should have as much fun as you possibly can. You have every right to upgrade yourself. You should not have to seek permission to do so. You are simply making positive changes in your life.

Making positive changes should be acceptable in everyone's lives. You only live once so while you have the opportunity ... UPGRADE!

It doesn't matter if you are a man or a woman, you can upgrade. If you are a man, go to the barber and get a fresh haircut. No matter where you live there is a barber or beauty shop. My friend Leroy who is overseeing Supercuts in Hawaii tells how people look so happy after getting a fresh haircut. If you are a woman, let your man have that beard or shave that beard and how about you get some new style underwear? Once you put those on, you will feel like a new woman. Upgraded ... yeah ... Upgraded. Like an orgasm in the back seat of a Buick. (Let's go find a smooth Buick)

Didn't know how good it would feel to be upgraded, huh?

Ok then, when you start upgrading yourself you have this feeling like you are a new person. And you wonder why you had not noticed the difference. Well, don't worry about yesterday...you have tomorrow to make it through ...because you've got things to do (laughing).

You are eating better and losing weight. You're wearing makeup and sporting a fresh new haircut. Gentlemen, you're pants are well fitted and your shirt slimly straight. You are looking good in your upgrade. Now, what level are you on?

Oh ... you didn't know we had levels, huh? That is too funny. Yes, there are levels. When you first realize you are making changes, you are at **Level One: Genesis —The Beginning.**

Then, once you start physical changes, such as working out or doing routine exercises, you graduate to the next level. **Level Two is Job —The Struggle**. At this level, you will experience a lot of what Job experienced, such as losing things and the people you love. A fight to change is not always easy. What if you have to quit smoking? That can be very difficult. This stage is the hardest, giving up things that you have always loved and used to have in your life. Eliminating people that stunt the growth, you are aiming to accomplish.

Upgrading isn't easy peoples so get your armor on . . .

Level Three is the stage of Psalms 23 —Prayer. You just want to pray your way through all these dang changes, Goodness. Who do you think can handle all this stuff? You got me eating better, losing weight and trying not to get this hair wet because I got things to do.

So, I'm upgrading. Now what? What do I do with my life? I left the man, got a new dog, chased off a friend or two, and I think I'm looking rather cute or handsome... Now what?

I mean if you want to know the truth... now I'm bored. All this upgrading and eliminating stuff and people give you more of your life back. You kind of feel like you is missing something. Yeah, really you are ... drama and crap. You have saved some money, made more money, added more time to your schedule and you look great. And gentlemen, may I add that new haircut and the sports car is making you look rather tasty. Even those jeans with those new style loafers, I'm digging it.

So why are you sitting there waiting for me to answer that question for you? Now what? What do you think; now what? You go out there and find some happiness for yourself. Create some fun stuff to replace the crappy stuff. Live life like it's supposed to be lived. You are officially Upgraded, so what are you waiting for. You have now jumped into the last level.

Level Four is **Revelations —The End and New Beginning.** Now you are on the road to complete the process for the rest of your life. You can keep the weight off, keep the smile on your face, live to be happy all the time... all the time. You are now able to live your life in such a way that the new process is an easy process that you can keep and adopt in your life. You have done great work and made great sacrifices once you have reached the final stage. You will never be the same. According to the 'Summer B' by-laws, one must be proud of whom you've become. By the power invested in me, you have been officially Upgraded!

In Summer's World ...

Sitting here writing about a totally different subject and I started to wander off and reflect. It's three o'clock in the morning, and I have an epiphany. This seems to be happening to me a lot lately. People say I have changed. To that I say, thank goodness! I was worried for a minute they were going to say something bad. Well, maybe to them it was bad but to me ... I was glad. I'm not supposed to stay the same. I am supposed to grow and advance. Gain knowledge and understanding. Be a better woman than I was before. I am supposed to be different.

You see, life is about moving on to the next level, upgrading your life, exploring what is out there in the world, living for today, with and in the best way. Advancing in your career, raising children to be adults and learning all that you can learn out of life.

If we do not learn the lessons that are presented to us, we can stay in our situations much longer than need be. I am trying to learn all that I can learn from every one of you that is ever in my circle of life. I want to advance to the next level. I want to grow up and be the best that I can be.

I am willing to be different in order to enlarge my territory. Share with the world my happiness and sunshine because that is what I am called to do. I want to stand out amongst the crowds and make people stare. Why?

I will always smile- people think it's odd that someone smiles as much as I. I try to be positive and happy in my life. I want to project happiness to others as much as possible. One smile can save someone's life. One simple hello can make someone's day.

I will always be kind to everyone including strangers- people freak out at my kindness and generosity. I make sure to be kind to someone always, especially total strangers. It's not always about giving money... what about giving one of your blessings.

I will always strive to be better; wanting to be a better mother, daughter, teacher, and friend. I will always want to learn all that I can learn in my life and go over and beyond what I am called to do.

Upgrading is never easy, and you will experience this for yourself once you start making those changes. People will disappear from your life, or people will come into your life. Whatever does happen will be a result of enhancement which is always a good thing; so do not feel as if you made the wrong decision to change.

It is not your fault that others cannot welcome the new you if that is the case. Everyone should always be happy for someone who has made positive changes in their life. That is a great accomplishment and cannot be made by everyone.

Again, starting small makes the transitions easier than not. Start with new underwear, then a new haircut and a new pair of shoes. Starting small is essential so that you don't over-do it. While you are upgrading yourself, you are also upgrading your finances too, but again, do not overspend in the upgrade.

Try looking at your local thrift stores and flea markets before you hit the mall and spend big money. Try and support your local mom and pop stores. They need community support more than the big franchises.

You don't need a million dollars to upgrade, in fact, you don't even need a dime. What you do need is…the right frame of mind. When your mind is ready and receptive to change, you can change and upgrade anything about you.

It doesn't take money to smile in public or walk with your shoulders held high. To be a born again human being simply means to bring forth positive change my friend ... to bring forth positive change!

Remembering to ...

- Change your life in a positive way ... upgrade

- Learn to like new things

- Learn from others as well as teach others as you learn

- Want to be different, desire to change

- Always be proud of who you are

- Create an oath to yourself to be yourself, one of change and love

- Grow in a positive direction

- Lose weight if you need to

- Listen to music - music heals your soul and create happy thoughts

- Make an effort to eat better, healthier and fresh

NOTES: *Remove the mask, step out of purgatory living ….*
artwork by Mario Sanchez

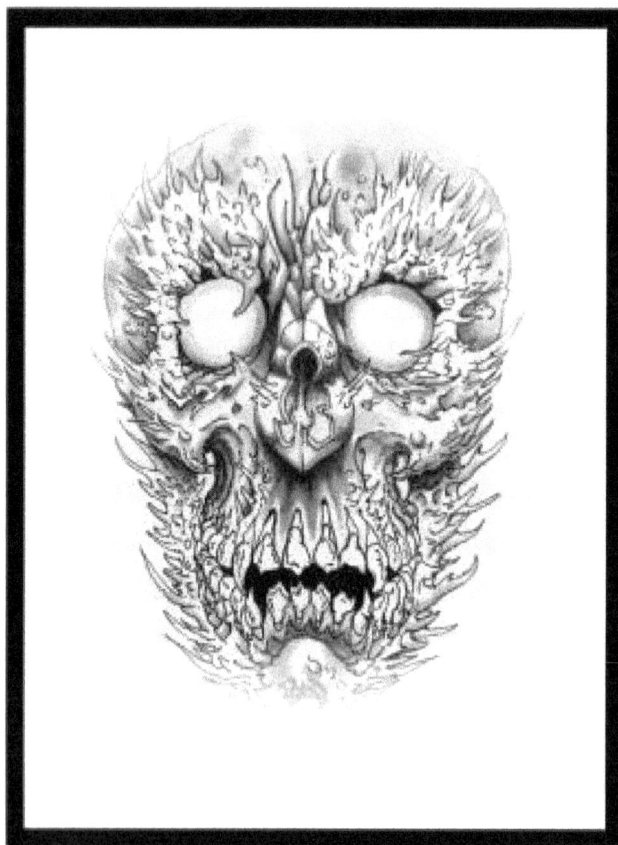

Mario Sanchez

5 Smoothly Polished

Now that you are Upgraded, you have to show that shine that comes from the polish you just received. You are different, and everyone can see it, kind of like a glow.

You know everyone has to make sacrifices towards stepping out of Purgatory ... life is what we make it and if we want to be happy, we have to make ourselves happy. Happy doesn't mean that you have to run around trying to change the world or laughing all the time. It is being content with what you have and making the best of everything in your life. It's changing your attitude about how you go through life and choosing to be happy, choosing contentment and understanding. If you add some patience, then you have the best five-star recipe ever created.

You are smoothly polished. You have the mindset of change and have flourished into a great person. Not to say you were not already, but if you can see in your view master slide (lost in purgatory) of which you were before you made the changes, you can see that you are a better person. Anything new in your learning of life establishes the official seal of better. We can feel so unworthy sometimes, and we have to change that attitude as well. We are worthy of better. Anything more than what we woke up with is considered greater or better whichever the vice.

In this polished process, you have to remember that it's not over. Every day you have to fight to be happy. Every day you have to want to stay out of Purgatory. People will want to make you lose your religion, but you have to keep it moving. No one should steal your joy and your sunshine. It is your right to carry it everywhere you will be.

Hey, send it ahead. I have lived my life in such a way that when my name appears or is said, sunshine and happiness shows out. That's how I send mine ahead. I give others the abundance of my happiness through my kindness and gratitude for their friendship or relations. I share happiness everywhere I go. I try to find something nice to say to someone throughout my day. I don't have to make a conscious effort to do so, but maybe you do. Compliment someone on their hair or shoes, even if it is not your style. Hold the door open for someone. Pay the toll for the person behind you. Do something on a regular that shows that you care about yourself and others in your circle.

I want to know that you have my back and that you care about me as a person. You have to care about people in action and not just in thought. That is part of loving who you are. You want others to be loved as well. One small thing can change someone's life, a simple hello on a rainy day, small sacrifices. It's like being the lead actress or actor in your own life. You want the perfect performance.

To get that standing ovation at the end, you have to work your butt off to practice and perform on a daily basis. Life is an everyday play. You have to play a part in every way, from home to church, the grocer, and the dry cleaner. You have to play a role to every person that you meet.

What will your audience think of your work? Will they give you thumbs up or down? Polished or not it should be part of our everyday makeup. Being a better person comes with a lot of duties. Sometimes you want to give up and just not care anymore, but you have to keep pushing forward. You have to get up every day and say I want to live. I want to live today. And take it one day at a time, and TODAY is our day. That's all we can do. We only have control over ourselves. We can only live for today. Yesterday is gone and tomorrow may not arrive and today is all you can live for. Today!

I love my polish; People compliment me on it daily. I represent happiness and sunshine everywhere I go. From my feet to my head, and I don't spend a lot of money to do it. It may not cost you one red cent.

I'm trying to tell you how; I hope you are paying attention. I would love for you to understand what your worth is. Man or woman, you have the right and deserve to be happy.

And you have to make sure that you are in charge of it. If someone else is in charge of your happiness, you are not going to be happy. If you allow anyone, even your spouse/friend to be in charge of what makes you tick, what makes you tick will be a time bomb.

You will tick and tick until you explode. It should be a joint effort if you have a spouse or partner. Everything you do should come from the both of you. Even if you have to take turns. No one should feel that they are living the other person's life, or living in the marriage or relationship alone.

You will feel so resentful for the whole relationship and end up bailing out faster than you fell in. Prevent unnecessary things in your life. Know what you want and what you are willing to sacrifice. You have a shine that people want, and when you allow others to color your sun, then you eventually can lose that shine in the darkness.

No one will talk about it when you walk by or call. When people see your name, they won't even raise a smile. You will be, lost, in the Purgatory of living, again.

Don't do it! Now if you can listen to the words that are coming out of my fingertips you will be successful in the pursuit of happiness.

Happiness is what you make it ... Point, blank ... period!

How do you think you are sitting here shinning. You got up every day, and you made it happen. You have to tell people how they will treat you. How do you do that, by treating yourself that way first? You have first to treat yourself the way you want others to treat you. And when they don't treat you with the respect that they should, then you can let them know, either by not doing business with them or losing them as a friend or family member. Some people you just have to love and respect from a distance.

Whatever the case may be, you have first to love you, respect you and care for yourself before others will do so. It's the way life is.

I don't understand why my shine is so bright. That means I have done great things? Am I so anointed with happiness that you need sunglasses to block the rays?

I love this new stage in my life, finding out who I am and who I want to be. The whole process can make you a little nervous, but change is good. If you have been respectful and obedient in all that you do, then you should be ok.

I can see your glow from here. How happy do you want to be? Because you know, you can just keep it going. Help others to be happy. Most people in life have to be taught how to be happy. You can start with family and then friends or however you see the need. You will discover that a lot is missing out of our lives.

You can start a game club, everyone come together once a week or month and play games together for fun. Go out shopping with a group of people. Make it fun, have lunch.

There are so many ways that you can share your glow. Everyone can see you now and knows you are different. Most of them want it too. Most people will be afraid to ask how you became happy. I mean…What kind of conversation is that? "So Mariah, how did you become so happy?" Yeah… so, you have to make sure not to keep it to yourself, or you have broken the covenant 'Thy shall not keep thy happiness to thyself.' You have to get out there and do it. But for the most part, you won't have to make a conscious effort. Watch how easy it will be for you since you have become so happy.

You do have to remember that life's problems and things will interfere and try to steal your happiness but you can't let it. We will always, always, go through things in life. It is how we go through it that determines our outcome. And I need to be happy. So, once you start shinning, people will wonder and watch you. They will envy you and want to steal your happiness. It's up to you how that ends up. You can allow what people say and do to steal your happiness or you can understand the fact that those kinds of people will always exist and brush that right off into the wilderness.

You don't have time …
Keep it moving. Stuff will hurt, and you have the right to be angry, but don't let it control you, keep your shine. You are Upgraded. Once you know better, you do better a wise man once said, as I am singing… "Go ahead and hate on me… cause I'm gone do me"!

When you are upgraded people will have those mixed reactions as to how they feel about you. First, they may not like the new you because they may not have a new them, so do not be surprised that you don't have a fan club. People generally hate shiners… it's just a shame but true. They do not want to be around people that shine but who cares, the more you shine, the more you may be able to convert some of those same people into shiners themselves. We are always teachers, and if someone keeps smiling at me every day I eventually will do the same if even to be a front but at least I'm doing it, and one day it may even be real…. See, every bit of happiness can help anyone!

Being smoothly polished is not something everyone can accomplish. You have to want to be Upgraded; you have to want to be changed, and honestly, you have to have the money or resources to do so.

Once you do change, that's when you get polished. It's like college graduation. Some of us may never graduate but hey, some of us will. It's just a matter of wanting to … again, I cannot stress that enough. Leroy over at SuperCuts shares with us (social media) about the program they have that helps the underprivileged or those in need. Visit their website on the news tab to read about what they are doing in the various community projects. What a blessing to be a part of such a wonderful and positive team of people. https://www.supercuts.com/about-supercuts/news/cuts-for-a-cause.html
NOW EVERYONE CAN SHINE! When you can get your hair done male or female, you can feel much better about yourself.

Nothing in life will ever happen to you or for you if you do not first want it. Once you have a desire to have it … anything can and will be yours. Don't sabotage your happiness and sunshine. Don't stand in the way of your glory.

You have a right to shine and be as polished as you need and want to be in this life right now!

We make excuses so much that we believe them ourselves. Why can't we be upgraded, different, happier, funnier, prettier, more handsome or just about anything else we want to be? Why do we make it so hard on ourselves to be better people?

You want to change your job yet you won't fill out the application for a new one. You want to ask your spouse to lose weight with you, but you won't ask because you think they will say no, but you have not asked and so what anyway. The point is that things will never change for us if we first don't think it, secondly to want it and thirdly to act on acquiring it. Figure out what you want and learn how to ask for it and get it!

Being smoothly polished is believing in yourself first and if the rest of the world doesn't, then so be it. That is not what matters in your life. What matters in your life is being comfortable with who and what you are right now today and making the right moves to stay in the comfortable life yet always advancing into a better you with each blink of your eye. Why would you live any other way?

As you begin your new journey, you will meet new people and with meeting new people you have new opportunities to be the new you. No one has to know you were any different before today. If you are making your necessary daily changes, everyone should be happy to see the enhancement.

I know when you look in the mirror you should remember it's not about how we look, but who we see on the inside of us and that reflects in the posture and position of our face. The posture of your face tells the world who you are and how happy you are.

``What does your facial posture reflect? It reflects posture and position.

Looking in the mirror starts as a tool to make sure that your face is free of unnecessary things but as time advanced it was used as a tool to see how beautiful or ugly one was at that moment in time. Understanding that we have no control over how or to whom we were born to will help you to not care about the features you see when looking in the mirror but simply that all is in order when looking in the mirror.

You can get chiropractic care for your spine, feet, face, and neck. When your spine is in line, everything will run fine, including your facial features. Chiropractic care helps boost your immune system, eliminate pain and correct issues you may be suffering from like sinus, diabetes, high blood pressure and more. When you feel better, you feel beautiful, inside and out.

Beauty will be what we make it to be. It doesn't matter where you come from, or who you are, what matters is the way you present yourself and the manner of which you speak. The key here is to know that it's always about respect. Respect who you are right now today and respect others the way they are.

No one has to call or visit you if they do not like who you are as a person. Everyone has a choice, and everyone has a reason. It's their right just as it is yours, but if you know you are properly living your life then your feelings will not hurt to the proper and appropriate rejection that is not rejecting to you but towards you. Don't take it personally is the bottom line, for you were not born to be projected into everything and everybody. There has to be a rejection button so just know this and keep it moving ... Next!

If you wanted to make changes in your life, that's a wonderful thing. If you were forced into making changes, well think about why? Why is it that we fight so hard towards necessary change? My grandmother after 40 years had to replace her toilet and you would have thought someone stole her entire retirement account.

We know we need a new toilet, but we will fight it for whatever the reason just because of its change. New money to be spent, a new seat to get used to ... it's like losing your favorite dog and having to pay for it at the same time.

Keeping yourself polished after going through so much and so many necessary changes will be hard. You have to smile when you may not want to smile, and you may have to say hello to someone you may not necessarily want to, but as the new, you arrive... so does your frame of mind. See, while you will always see a smile on my face and hear it in my voice, I sometimes do not want to smile, but because I so love people, I do it anyway. It's part of my DNA, who I was born to be.

Everyone doesn't skip when they walk or smile when they talk but you can if you want to. If others see your polish, they will want it too even if they pretend not to.

Always be true to yourself and others will follow... again if they don't, it's their loss and not yours. You have some new underwear on, a fresh new haircut and a new attitude. Cost you all but $25 bucks, and you feel like a million! It's ok to go further if you want to... some clients purchase an entirely new wardrobe but remember that you are dressing differently than before so ask for a little help in doing so. You can also purchase yourself a new car if you have the funds. Do what your budget allows you to upgrade without losing your savings or getting into deeper debt.

We should not be acquiring new debt we should be eliminating old ones. Polish me please if it's like that. Why would you not want to be smoothly polished, male or female, single or married? It's not about how much money you have or what your status is, it's about making a difference in your circle, and that difference is being happier people!

Making Wonderful ...

After all that you have done and become you should feel like a million bucks or do you? Sometimes when we make changes for the better, it may seem to come off as the worse. There are times when you will feel lonely and empty because you have gotten rid of all the foolish and useless people and things in your life.

You may have to go to the movies alone and be happy about it. If you want fun, you will have to create it as you go along. What exactly do you want from your life? Do you know what kind of life you want?

For you to be Upgraded you must learn that to feel that wonderful feeling, you must create that wonderful feeling, like creating your own game of life and not the game of others.

I keep a photo of the real board game of life as a reminder that every day that I am a part of the world I have to, in turn, play the game that others have created. Happiness will be what we make it, at least the part we have control of. If you could create your own game of life, what would it be?

For the most part, wonderful comes when you learn to control today and today only. We cannot control yesterday for it has already passed and we do not know what tomorrow will bring for it may never come so we can only live in the present which is today, and today we only have control over ourselves so let's create some wonderful. Today… for you! Wonderful comes when we are ready for it to come … point blank period!

It's for us to want and then to act out accordingly as each day comes and goes. Some of us are trying to live in the future so much that we can't live for today!

Today is all that matters … what are you doing in your today? Some people don't know how to find their happy spot, there some kind of wonderful. Some people fight being Happy!

Some people create the miserable life they are in and to a degree they love it if there is no drama than life is no good, in their twisted mind. What kind of life is that?

Wonderful is waking up in the morning and just happy to be alive for one more day. It's about not what time you have to get up to start your days but about the fact that you have a day to wake up to is the bonus. Everyone was not able to wake up this morning, whether you think that's a good thing or not. It's a gift. Wonderful can be having good food to eat today or being able to go to work. Everyone does not have a job and cannot secure food for their family.

Smiling is a part of my makeup; it's part of my every day. No one has to make me smile; in fact, I try to extend my smile to others … that's my wonderful. I can do things for myself, and that in itself is wonderful. There are so many things in life that can be you're wonderful, but you have to take the time to sit back and see the wonderful things in your today. Today is what we live for.

I often go to the bookstore and play around in different sections, reading on different subjects and meeting new people in life. I walk around the waterfront and allow myself the blessing of enjoying the beauty of the day, even if it's raining.

Wonderful can be whatever you need it to be as long as you make it a point to create it in your mind first and then to implement it in your everyday.

Life is what we make it … look at your view master and see what your past says about your happiness and your wonderful. Once you make up in your mind that you want it… you can have it! How wonderful do you want to be? How wonderful can your life be you ask? Have you ever really evaluated your life and why it is not the way you want it to be?

Well, we suggest you do that earlier in the book, but it's something you should do on a regular basis. No need to be upset about a detoured life, simply re-evaluate it and redirect it to where it should be. It's never too late.

If you need to know why it's that way, write that down as well but focus on the change and what you can do to change the situation. Remember you only have so much control but if we are doing our part than our outcome will be better than not.

Wonderful is sitting in the living room with no cable listening to your local radio station with a smile on your face because today you live and not the fact that you cannot watch television. Mind thoughts will determine how we live our lives. It's how we create our wonderful.

If you believe you can do something, you most likely can if you want to and try to. If you make yourself smile when you want to frown, you will learn to create peace when you go through the different transitions in your life.

I have a friend, Marisela. She is always happy. She knows how to make wonderful. Always creating fun things for her children to do and always making her life and her days better days. She's such a gift to watch and be friends with for she has a concern for people, but most importantly she takes care of herself first. She is very talented and always shares her talents with others. She's my paralegal and the best at what she does, so if you ever need one to assist you in legal matters, let me know. But again, wonderful is what we make it, and like Marisela, you have choices to make it what you need it to be for you and your family.

Your wonderful will be determined by your mind and how well you can control it. You have to make a conscious effort to do things differently than before. Life is like a play; we act accordingly to the way the world puts on the show. Each part of our lives is like entering a play. You may have to switch roles as you go along. Today you may have to smile at someone at work that you don't care for and say things a different way than you normally would. Just like in a play you learn your lines and act accordingly.

Your wonderful comes when you get your lines right, studying your script and being the lead actor or actress in your own life. Again, life will be what you and you alone make it.

Remembering to ...

Make it wonderful ... Make it you!

- Be polished and proud

- Continue to polish you

- Mindset of change

- Don't sabotage your happiness

- Do not allow others to steal your happiness

- Do things that are pleasing to you

- Make Wonderful thoughts, feelings, and things

Only you can keep yourself polished daily with your actions! Remember not to put too much into life daily chores. Sometimes to keep the peace, you may need to eliminate participating in some things. You may have to take a rain check on a few events in life so that you can keep your shine. If you don't have your mind right, money and people can destroy what you have worked so hard to achieve ... simply believe in YOU!

NOTES:

6 Dance Into A Better You

When I was lost in Purgatory Living, I gained lots of weight. Like fifty to sixty pounds of weight! Ok... so I was really lost. We have determined that factor. Moving on…

After I rediscovered myself, I decided that I wanted to lose weight. Once I made that decision, it was easy. I started walking and I walked for about an hour every day of the week. Some of you may not be able to walk seven days of the week, but you can walk as much as your time allows you to.

I walked seven days a week for a total of seven hours. Once I got used to walking I graduated myself up to one hour and twenty minutes. I added the extra time by walking to the park in my neighborhood which was an extra twenty minutes of walk time.   Once I got to the park, I walked all the way around it once and then I go to the swings and swing for about ten minutes.

What a workout that is. It is so much fun as well. I really love going to the park. You do not need to be a child to do it, just courteous of the children that may be in the park at the same time as you. No stealing swings…lol!

When I could not make it out on the trail I walked in my back yard. Walking in circles for 20 minutes was great. The need to keep up the program is essential so if you can do it in the yard, the family room etc, as long as you are keeping it moving.

So during this time I was really doing it, lost a little weight, about fifteen pounds in one month. And then I ended up in the hospital with a back problem. End result: a severe bulging disc in my lower back, the month before I fell in my kitchen. Hurt my knee and I thought that was it. I am in pain and my life has changed. I was all happy and stuff and now I have a back issue worse than what I had already. I mean really, I am just trying to be happy. I do not want to keep having to go through all this stuff of people and things trying to steal my shine...

I did not let that stop me needless to say. I kept it moving. I could not walk as much with the back being in so much pain so I stayed at home and I put a record on the record player and I danced. I danced myself from a size sixteen into a size eight dress on a bad day.

Let me tell you, I had the best time of my life. I discovered so much in me that I didn't know was trapped in this bunch of nothing spinning in my head. I was home alone, the ex-husband was at work, the son was always gone, and so I took advantage of the time. I would lock the door to the den and party all by myself. I might even have a glass of wine. And I danced and danced and danced the night away. I would dance for up to about two hours some nights.

I remember some nights listening to my favorite DJ, Tony Bear, and the valley radio station. They play old school music from back in the day. Tony Bear was always on the radio with all of my favorite music from my era. I would have a blast all by myself.
    Then I heard the radio station was visiting a local venue in town for a happy hour live on the radio on a Friday night and *oh boy!* was it on. It's been about five years since I had my first dance too. Listening to that radio station helped motivate me to go out by myself, dance my worries away and meet new people along the way.

It became such a great end of the week event with all my new happy hour friends; it helped motivate me to become a better me. I was able to dress up however I chose to dress, go out and just dance for fun, no other point intended. Everyone who follows Tony Bear became friends so there was always someone to talk to and dance with, male or female, just a great group of people to know and meet.
    Motivation from music, people, and dance is the key to helping you become a better you ... daily.

Dancing at home was allot fun for me. I wore my workout pants with high heels, comfortable high heels that made me feel sexy and were sturdy enough to be comfortable enough to dance in. I also put on makeup and fixed my hair just a little, made myself look a little sexy. I felt sexy, even though I felt ugly. The point was to Upgrade myself, and so I did. My outer appearance is not very important, but I think it helps when trying to attempt such a large task in life.

Doesn't have to be anything major but allowing yourself the privilege of simple beauty is priceless and well deserved... go for it! I danced to anything and everything. It was the best hour or two of my life.

When I was done ... I put away the records, tossed out the wine bottle and ditched the high heels. No one would ever know what I was doing in there.

Then one day ... BAM! I stepped out of the room, and I was a Baywatch babe. My whole world changed.

Helping people to refocus their self in life . . .

You don't have to need to lose weight. You don't have to have a perfect life not to participate. It's about upgrading no matter what level in life you are. Upgrading is something everyone in every walk of life can participate in. There is something about you that can use enhancing. Not to say it's wrong or broken, but simply enhance me. See...easy! E-n-h-a-n-c-e M-e!

No one even has to know you're doing it is the fun part. You can change the way you answer the phone, or give a friend your house number instead of your cell phone, make it personal. That's being a better friend, a better person. That is upgrading from who you were before you started.

You can start answering calls versus letting them always go to voicemail, which is being a better person. Taking the extra time to ensure the person on the other end of the phone is taken care of. They took the time to call you unless they are a bill collector, it's all good.

Now dancing can be so therapeutic. You don't have to need anything to want to listen to music and possibly with friends and dance. I can hear music anywhere and want to dance right where I stand. No matter where it is. I can hear some great music in the grocery store and just start moving. Once you start listening to music, you will not want to stop.

It is such a healer of all ills. You end up finding music that fits the theme of your life at that current moment in time. It is amazing how healed you become in such a short period. It may bring out some stuff you didn't know exist. You can be going through a divorce, a bad relationship, your job just sucks, or you just got fired. Or the best part of all is that you cannot need anything and this just adds such an enhanced feeling of contentment to your soul.

It's like an orgasm on the beach, just you and the one of your dream on the beach of your choice while the ocean beats a beat that only you can hear.

You are feeling that music and you are rocking your body to the beat and you can feel it like the magic marker just appeared and started writing your life script. Once you start dancing ... you are different. You are a little happier.

You are rocking in the car, bopping to the beat in the work cubicle. You fill those empty spots with music. You may even want to see a concert or hit a dance club. Have fun and just dance. Just Dance!

You will discover that certain moves you make will allow you to lose certain fat in different parts of your body

Dancing is such a spirit lifter. It changes the way you think. And in turn, changes the way you live.

You are a better employee, friend, parent, lover...

Imagine being a better lover. For the most part, once you start dancing, you may want to have sex more than you already do. See, its part of the upgrading. Once you start making yourself happier, thus the feeling of sex can come into play.

I am gigging my butt off. I am having the time of my life! If I don't hear music, I am not the same.

When my back is not cooperating, I take it slow. Sometimes I move just a little, or I may have to take a break. At times I may have to miss a week or two, but I will start again. You have to continue. You cannot let anything steal your shine.

It's up to you to get up and dance again. I take care of myself, so I can enjoy my life. You have to make a vow to take care of YOU. No one will do it for you, and you are the only one in control of it.

Some of you may want to sit in a chair and dance while sitting. That is also a lot of fun to do. There are days when I have to do just that. You can do that at work, if you cannot move about, you can put on some earphones and dance right there in your chair.

Rejuvenate your spirit ... You have to find a way to find peace. Take your break and dance for fifteen minutes. If SummerB hasn't danced her way into your company's board meeting, maybe you should look into it. On the website, you can find information.

I just feel such joy when I am dancing. My family thought I was crazy. My son would make fun of me all the time. You see, once I got my new revelation, my son had never seen his mom in the way that she was becoming. I used to be skinny and cute and funny and fun and had a lot going on back then, but he didn't remember. He was too young. So he is flipping his lid right about now. The girls ... they love it. The granddaughter was ecstatic to see grandma change for the better.

My son said one day that all he knew was that he wanted his mom back ... I was playing the music so loud he would be upset. He would try to turn the music down, and I would turn it back up. He didn't understand what I was going through. He was eighteen at this time, and I was gearing up for an empty nest. Things were falling into place —one dance at a time.

I went out and danced maybe once a month. I try to make sure I go out and dance as to meet new people and just dance. That's why I started the dance classes so that you can motivate each other. Even if you're not in it for the weight loss, be in it for fun. I mean how fun is it when you can dance with some of the same people regularly.

You can invite your girlfriends over or if you're married or have couples as friends, invite them over, and you all can dance together. How much fun would that be? That is a great way to introduce it. Make a party out of it. And do it a couple of times a month. You can do it on your own a couple of times a week. For some of you, you may dance every day. It's up to you.

Dancing can be a lot of fun. You can dance off of any music for any amount of time, your dance, your way. It's that simple!

No excuses! According to family and close friends, I cannot dance at all. They say I have no rhythm. I really don't. Ask my children. They laughed. I laughed as well...after I lost fifty pounds dancing!

The whole point is that you can make any little moves to music and you will make a difference. I cannot say it enough. It's not just for weight loss; it's for good old-fashion fun! So when do you want to get started? If you already dance at 'the spot' on the weekend, why not do it at your spot during the week? It is just a few minutes of your time. Once you dance for five minutes, you will eventually keep adding time because it is so much fun. It is not the same as club dancing. I would love to dance with you.

Life is what we make it. Go out there and have fun. It does not matter who or what we are. What matters is that we take the time to enjoy the fruits of our labor.

Upgrade yourself into a better you. You are already great, but a dab of premium grade couldn't hurt at all. Ooohh ... look at you! The more you dance, the sexier you look. "Come here...let me see what you are working with."

Mindful Eating

It's not just dancing. Try to make it a whole lot of fun. When you have made up your mind that you are ready to make a change in your life, anything is possible. The possibilities are great and unlimited, especially when losing weight. Music is the key to healing all souls, and when you listen to it daily, music can help you become a healthier and happier you!

The first steps to Dance Into a Better YOU are...

1. **Eat healthier**. You may want to consider cutting out fast food. If you are always on the go and able to bring your lunch to work, put a cooler in the back of your vehicle daily so that you have access to water, fruit and a sandwich when needed. It will help you to not stop at the fast food diners. Fast food will always be the reason you gain or keep weight on.

2. **Eat breakfast daily**. i.e., Oatmeal, Cheerios, Cream of Wheat, etc. Eating a great breakfast is Ok. Take it lightly on the syrup and anything that makes you groggy, like pancakes and waffles.

3. **Eat your bigger meals during the day**. You will have the rest of the day to burn it off versus eating it late in the evening and gaining fat.

4. **Carry and eat snacks**. It is very important to eat snacks between your meals. No need to be fat-free or have bland snacks but pay attention to health. You want to eat what you like without making it difficult for yourself. Keep it simple ...

5. **Drink lots of water**. You may want to consider NOT drinking soda if you are a soda drinker. People who stop drinking soda can see the results instantly in energy and weight. Diet soda makes a lot of people thirsty and hungry, causing you to eat and drink more so, don't confuse yourself trying to consume diet products instead.

It's up to you what you end up consuming. The more I danced, the hungrier I became. My dancing and happy attitude advanced my metabolism, and I burned more calories without even realizing it.

I would appear to be hungry when it was time for me to eat.
Something you are not used to doing. Your body is used to creating a day by day schedule for activities and eating. It would benefit you to put yourself on a light schedule, and at least know when and what you are eating today.

Don't forget the cooler! You will be so grateful you packed one. Just wait until you notice how much more energy you'll have by eating healthier. Eating fast food makes you feel sluggish and slow. Who wants more energy? *Me... Me... I do!*

Remembering to ...

- Care about what you put into your precious body

- Take a cooler when you can with fresh fruit and vegetables

- Drink plenty of water daily

- Make sure to eat all of your meals at the time they are to be consumed

- Create a schedule if you need to as to the intake of calories, but don't put too much into it

- Enjoy eating yet be mindful of it

- Try to buy fresh food when you can so that you are eating healthier

- Eliminate fat from your diet

- Eliminate fast food from your diet

Don't create a diet or use pills, simply use mindful eating by; change the time you eat as well as eat smaller portions. Your body will adapt to the new schedule and proportion within a six week period. Keep eating smaller meals to train your stomach to want less.

The less you eat, the less it will want. A large saucer is great compared to a large plate. Talk to your doctor if need be but just eat what you like without eating too much and at late hours.

Life is for the living if we can do it appropriately. If you need help from a profession, do seek help but try to do things on your own first, to see how much power you possess, once you have your mind right.

NOTES:

7 Strutting Your Stuff

Now that you have been dancing, male or female, you feel different. You feel a little sexier than you did before. You have a different strut. You dance here and there. You are grooving to the beat anywhere you hear it which is very sensual, and you feel like you are on top of the world.

You have some heavy pep in your step. Now that you are upgraded into a better you, you can enjoy the benefits of it all. Look over there at that lady looking at you. She thinks you are glowing and she is probably right. Just thinking about upgrading can throw the glow on. I don't know about you, but I try to upgrade on a regular basis.

I was walking in the electronics store looking for a camera for my every day. A salesman walked over to me and asked if I needed any help. I looked into his eyes, and for a brief moment, he stood there frozen in time. He answered my question, and I walked off with my skirt swaying this way and that way to the rhythm of his heartbeat and he was about to fall over when his colleague came over and nudged him on the arm. He darn near had to wipe the drool off his face.

That new strut you got can hurt somebody. That new haircut you have is creating a shine people have never seen before. Even if you are a man, your stride is a little longer. You think your penis has grown some. That's how you are feeling. After being Upgraded, you feel like you can take on the world. Life is good. Things are better, even if they appear to be the same, your attitude about it is much different, happier and more understanding. Again, we will get angry, but we will know how to channel it better.

Keep strutting your stuff ... I know that's right. That dancing sure can make you look like a million dollars. I feel so good when I dance I feel like I am a professional. I just laugh at myself and keep it moving.

You have to know that when you control your happiness ... life can be good. Life is… you know what we make it.

I choose to be happy. I choose to live my life the way I want to live it, for me...

It's my time to change and glow . . . If it's not your time, don't be running around screaming it's your time, messing it up for everybody else. I want to keep my strut, shoot.

I like the way you Upgraded... looking all uppity and things. I don't know about you, but when I put on new underwear, I feel like the horniest woman on the block! I mean, a new piece of underwear can make you strut your stuff a little harder. Or…how about wearing a new bra with matching panties? You would probably do the mailman (if you're single) if he knocked on the door! (just a joke)

Men, when you get that fresh haircut and buy some new underwear, your penis may grow a couple of inches. Really, it does (in your mental mind.) If you think it, so shall it be!

Those underwear is squeezing those testicles just the way your woman does, or you wish one to be is making your strut turn the whole world on. You got the women staring at you, and the men are doing a double take. You are tearing up some stuff out there.

Lustfully tamed to the rhythm of your steps, you are controlling your environment and creating what the whole world is looking for. Everyone wants to be Upgraded. Everyone wants a new strut. The problem is that everyone does not know how to get it.

You ask, "So tell me Summer B…How do I get a new strut?" First, make up in your mind that you want a new strut, which means you want to be different. You want a larger penis, and you want to feel sexy.

Well, do you? I don't understand why there is even a question about whether you want to upgrade or not. How dare you even think that you would not want to be better than you already are? Everyone deserves to be enhanced, and so do you!

The only thing in life we have control over is ourselves. We control our happiness, sadness, and whateverness! No one else should have control over how we feel or what we do.

No one should be making us curse when we don't want to. You have a choice to remove those people and things from your life that is causing you to lose your blessings.

Try strutting your stuff after you have changed the way you answer people's questions, allowing the elevator to wait for someone even if you are in a hurry or holding the door for anyone at all. You will feel better about yourself once you start doing things that are different than the way you have always done them. The trip to the store is no longer just that anymore. You have held the door open for someone, and you even started a conversation with someone in line. That is two things that you would normally not have done, you have upgraded yourself in one trip to the store.

Now, can you do it again, how about making that a part of all of your trips? To the gas station, you can tell the attendant to have a great day. At the coffee shop, you can leave a tip and thank the clerk for helping you.

For some of us this is normal and can't imagine life without this... but for a portion of the world ... this here is something foreign and new, a learned experience. Wow... yes. Some people do not know how to be nice and happy. That too is how we lose ourselves in life, not taking the time to do little extra things that make a difference.

It's not just for the person that you are doing them for; it's also for you. It makes your spirit happier and brighter; it makes your purpose more fulfilling.

You don't need a doctor to tell you to lose weight. You don't need a friend to tell you that you need to change the way you dress. You already know these things you just choose to ignore it. Don't you want to strut your stuff a little, just a little?

A friend of mine, Leroy Thomas has the perfect strut. Leroy is a hair stylist, top of the line. He has his shop (Salon Manaz) in Richmond, California as well as making a world of change with Super Cuts, being located now in Hawaii. Leroy creates the kind of change that people need. He gives people the strut that is envied by all. He has a belief that everyone is beautiful regardless of their past for everyone deserves to feel upgraded, happy and free.

My friend Leroy comes from Richmond, Ca where he fell hard to his lowest moment but with faith and perseverance he made it a point to come out of his purgatory of living, and he made changes in his life that allowed him to step into a new beginning.

Never in a million years did he imagine that he would come out of purgatory and into a new world, and he especially didn't imagine that he would own one of the number one shops in his hometown. When you step into Salon Manaz it's like you are family, no matter where you come from or where you are going, Leroy to some is what President Obama or Trump is to others…. Hope for the future.

If Leroy can shine so bright like the sun after enduring so many failures, so can we. His strut is projected in his everyday life, his words, his smile, his actions and his tears of joy (no longer sorrows). You can find inspiration for many people you may know. And to look at Leroy Thomas now helping to grow a number one hair salon in Hawaii ... Super Cuts. When I look at Leroy on his social media page in Hawaii smiling and skipping into his work ....it makes my day. Join me in applauding Leroy for doing what some only dream of doing and being... Happy! "I just love God, people, life and just want to be HAPPY" - Leroy Thomas

When Leroy uses his hands to create magic in someone's world, he is filled with the desire to create more and more, one head at a time, one adventure at a time. The perfect example of purgatory living and stepping into a new beginning. He simply loves what he does and so can you.
And just so you know … a haircut or new style goes a long way. It does put more pep in your step. Instant happiness awaits you.

Imagine feeling like you just stepped out of a magazine, but you look the same as you did your whole life. Imagine that the sun shines at all times even on rainy days. Imagine that your life was still the way it is whether it is messed up or not but you see things differently and better. You can cope now and not panic; you can do things that you were not able to do before. Little things like saying no to a friend, or saving some money for a rainy day.
Your strut is getting bigger and bigger. And your attitude about life has great meaning. It means you want to be HAPPY! You choose to be happy.
We have choices in life, choices to make on a daily basis. When you open your eyes in the morning ... you have a choice to make; today I choose to be happy regardless of how the game is played. There are many games played at the same time in our lives, and we are key players.

We determine our outcome.

Do we curse people out today? Do I allow the lady at the carpool to make me angry? Do I let my boss bring me down? Or do I smile at the person who does me wrong... bring the carpool lady some muffins and compliment her on her suit. I can also start looking for another job if my boss is affecting my work habits. If you do not want to be somewhere or with someone, you have all the power to change it. Remember, once you change things, your strut becomes larger.

Choices, Chances, and Changes; you must make a Choice to take Chances or else nothing ever Changes. If you don't try new things, how will you be able to grow and prosper? How will you know what you want out of life is you don't take chances? As long as they are not life-threatening chances than just get out there and do it.

It is our civic duty to be better people. It is no longer acceptable to continue on the way we are. We have to take responsibility for ourselves in our life that we have created or allowed someone else to create. We have to step up to the plate and say that I am full, thank you! It doesn't mean that you take advantage of the fact that people now look at you better and give you more respect. Make sure not to disrespect anyone in your quest to a better you. You can float your boat without causing problems.

People should smile when they see you, not hate to see you coming. When I see my friend Leroy smiling, I smile and smile even more. It's a catchy fun kind of feeling when good people smile. We need that type of energy in our lives.

There are so many ways that we can make changes in our lives, changes that take almost no effort at all. Make an effort to smile, compliment someone or hold the doors open. Pay someone's toll or anything that will make a difference in someone else's life as well as your own. If it's not different, it's not an upgrade. Now get out there and strut your stuff! You deserve it!

Remembering to ...

- Strut Your Stuff daily, be happy with who you have become!
- Listen to music in your daily life; music heals the soul!
- Choose to be Happy from the moment you open your eyes
- UPgrade yourself daily
- Make necessary changes within your control
- Do something kind for others as part of your everyday
- Keep a list of goals and accomplishments

Strutting your stuff is a right that you have when you live your life in such a way that is deserved and earned. You have worked hard at becoming who you are as a people, and you deserve to live it accordingly. We are to reap what we sow, and if we are sowing good things, we deserve to have good things in life as a result.

Being better people is an everyday effort that we all have to work hard on a continuing basis to be. We are to learn the good of life and teach it to others. Strutting your stuff is a great feeling and should be continued throughout your journey in life by all means necessary.

Life is meant to be lived and to live today is a great blessing that is celebrated by the way we present ourselves to the world. Strut on!

NOTES:

8 Life and the Wonderful World of Work

You may wonder how in the hell can you upgrade yourself at work. You feel like you are going to go postal on someone as is. How in the world will I be able to smile and be happy with so many hormones under one roof at one time? *Ooohh... Pick me! Pick me!*

Choose to do one or two things... smile and be happy regardless of what is said or what goes on or find another job. It's that simple. Or is it?

Ok, so finding a job is not that easy and when you want to smack someone who really deserves it, well let's just say that it takes a strong hand of a higher being to hold some of us back. But I want to know one thing? Do you want to be happy?

Well, what are you going to do about it? I, myself, have always sought employment at places that were pleasing to me. Places that made me happy. Well, places that enhanced my happiness. I am in control of what and who makes me happy. I try to enhance the workplace by adding things that were cute. Try having fresh flowers in the office. Stop at the local farmers market or flower shop and pick up some fresh flowers once a week. That will brighten up any room and any atmosphere.

How about rearranging the furniture to your office? If you can't do that, add something like a photo or painting. Put one of those desk games or fixtures so that you can distract yourself for a moment as needed. If you have a private office, bring a small radio that plays soothing music or makes it fun music depending on the boss. Music makes for better workers if you can listen to music while working, how much more work you can produce. Music is motivating and healing.

Making employees work together makes for a better team. A company in whole has one common goal, and that goal is to create revenue while helping the consumer. Every employee is supposed to be a team player. No one is different from the other. Each employee is a piece of the puzzle so why is it we are always at odds with each other. Ok, so we have different pieces of the puzzle, some more important than the other but the common goal remains the same.

I worked at Shattuck Autobody Center in Berkeley/Oakland, Ca and if you know body shops you would know that they are manly, for they are mechanical lol. I had to make the most of what I had. I loved my job. I left a large company that could have been a career for me to work at the body shop because it made me happy. I am awesome at everything I do, but the corporation couldn't provide me enough happiness. So to make due at the body shop, I wore cute things like coveralls and jumpsuits with boots that were made for a woman but fits in the manly scene just the same. It was a win-win. I loved my job, so I created my form of happiness.

Make your environment happier. Use bright colors to decorate. Use bright paper if you are only sending in-house information. If the company allows it for the outgoing than why not make life happier and fun, your clients and or co-workers may enjoy it. I know for me, it makes for a happier employee. Look at the different companies that already implement this like those big computer companies. They know that if you make your employees happy that they will give over and beyond what they are called to do.

Everyone does not want to share the happiness in the workplace! Why are companies so quiet and stiff, so grey and depressing? Well, you cannot always change the decor or the employees, but you can change your view of it all. You can change how you react to the people around you. You can change how you react to the situation that presents itself.

Your reaction determines your outcome, just as your attitude determines your latitude (as an eagle).

You have to choose not to go off on people. You have to choose to accept your position and simply work on changing it if you are unhappy. If that means look for employment elsewhere than that's what you need to do. You should not by any means, make everyone else unhappy because you are unhappy. You should not be trying to get other employees to sign on your bandwagon because you need a new job.

No... don't do that. Keep your mouth shut or do something about it. You can make some small changes without anyone even noticing, especially within yourself. Remember where the control lies, and you won't have any problems in life. As I heard on television, someone says... "You have lots of things to think about, but nothing to worry about." And that's real. You have to take the control back you have given to others and create your happiness in the workplace. Buy some plants, bring in some donuts, smile more and pay more compliments.

If no one appreciates that stuff ... keep doing it. Who cares what they think. You will continue to receive your blessings for being such a great person, and the blessing is your happiness.

You are not living with anyone else you are living for you. Always be true to yourself!

You do not have to be validated in the workplace or at home. If you know you can do the job better than your boss, well work hard and if that does not get you promoted than look for another position elsewhere. But always know that you are a blessing regardless of what others think of you. The workplace is a very hard place to live. It's a place with limited choices unless you own the company. You have no control over what goes on within a company, but you do have control over you and how you play the company game of life.

You see, in the wonderful world of work, there are many games and key players. Just like a football team. A basketball team and so on...

What is your position? Are you a loner? Let's look at what that position entails...

The workplace loner . . . is one who typically comes to work to do their job and does not participate in most workhouse activities. They don't hang out for lunch; they don't go out to lunch with the group.

This usually means a few things… Usually, it means that the loner has a way of life that is not like the others. Often it is for religious purposes or simple morals; they don't like company drama.

I remember not wanting to be a part of certain conversations at work because they lead to personal conversations and to keep it simple... I don't bring my personal self to work. So ... you call them loners, but they are simply good people that do not want to be included in workhouse confusion. That's what mixing personal life and work life can bring.

Then you have the show-off... The show off is one that always has their work done on time or early. The show-off volunteers for everything to please the boss and may even dress swanky ... an employee of the month every month, short dresses or expensive suits, always trying to be the pleaser, the person to take care of it all. And will step on everyone's toes to make it to the top only to die of a heart attack on their vacation. Oh well, so sorry for your loss. No need to say more about the show-off. We all know a showboater...

Oh... then there is the office hoe ... Yeah ... you know the one, the one that flirts with everyone.

She wears sassy clothing and always trying to please the men. The women despise her, and the package delivery man adores her. And I heard through ten grapevines that she slept with seven co-workers already this year. And now somewhere in the land of the free, it is legal to fire an employee if someone is a threat (too cute/sexy) to the sanction of your marriage/relationship/family. Ok ... What? Right! Ok sweetie, we have to let you go!

The office hoe also comes in a male version. He is the sweet talker, gets the ladies to buy him lunch and dinner as he smoothes talk them out of money or sex. He has sex with all the interns and the female employees. He is Mr. OMG I have to have him.

You have so many people under one roof that it can become impossible to be happy. Well, I can agree with that except saying that it doesn't have to last forever. Again, you have choices. You have a choice to go in there and do two hundred percent and go home and complain, or you can start participating and maybe making some suggestions and additions.

We are working together for the sake of our families. We are sacrificing our time and our talents for the sake of feeding the family. We have to have a place to live, and food to eat and the way to do that is through our work. If we can agree to work together... there is so much we can accomplish.

Everyone deserves to work in peace and harmony. Why does one purposely hurt you in the workplace, to better their career? Well, how far do they think they will get in life? Maybe their life will appear good now but in the end... not worth it.

As a business owner, I would rather see an employee helping others to succeed versus only helping themselves up the ladder. I would not promote an employee who is self-motivated and selfish. That means that the goal we are trying to accomplish as a company and family could be in jeopardy of destruction due to self-motivation. Some people strive on "by any means necessary" to get to the top. It's your call how your story ends.

Mine... I keep it moving. Doing over and beyond what I am called to do. But what if there is friction at work. How are you supposed to deal with that and remain a happy employee really? Well, sometimes there will be drama in the workplace. Learning how to address issues without confusion or madness. If you still can handle it, you will then have to move on, find happier employment elsewhere.

My best job and learning experience came from Mosher & Ellis Financial Planning (Lafayette, Ca) ... a job that I will remember for the rest of my life. They taught me so much about work and life that I carry that in my every day. I worked for that company as a secretary and assistant to the CEO for a few years. Mr. Mosher hired a professional (Patricia) to come in every Tuesday morning and teach us how to work together, accomplish our goals timely and to be better people individually and as a whole while creating bigger revenue for the company by improving our daily work ethics and habits.

Of course, we dreaded Tuesday mornings, but as we moved along, they became easier and anticipated. Every time I had to mail that check to Patricia for the company, I thought "what a waste of money," but as we grew, individually and together, I realized she wasn't getting paid enough. I felt I learned more than a four-year college graduate during that time.

The knowledge of life and expectancy is not given to everyone, and not everyone can teach it if they do carry it, so to have the exposure of such a great gift is PRICELESS! I may not remember what the best fund is to invest your money in, but I can assure you that I remember and implement what Patricia taught me in those Tuesday morning meetings! It's been fifteen years, and they still hold the Tuesday morning meetings...lol! Call and see.

You have control over yourself only, at all times. Utilize that control, make yourself happy regardless. Let them fire you over being overzealous. There are some of you right now under the text of my fingers that want to walk out of your job ... right now! I do advise that you talk it out with your spouse or whoever may be affected by your decision to say "take this job and shove it." You can then do what you need to do but make sure everyone is ok with it.

Why do we always want to knock out the boss? Because we have to train ourselves how to be employees but the owners do not get trained on how to be a successful owner. They lack more than we do the job. Again, you have to find the right fit. Don't jump into a job just to have a job if you can help it. Make sure it's as good a fit for you as it is for them.

I see people on a regular basis that come into the office and immediately start complaining. They drink too much coffee and stand around all morning. I don't understand that type of work ethic. The reason I don't understand is that you are getting paid to come in and do a certain and specific job.

You are old enough to understand all of that, yet you come to work and do not want to put your one hundred percent in. You may want to contribute about forty percent today, and tomorrow you have a funeral to go to so you are only going to put in about ten percent.

If that's you … it's time for a career change. You see, if you don't want to be somewhere, you don't have to. If you don't want to work for the company, then don't apply. Don't waste people's time and money. It's not going to make you happy; you are going to be miserable. If you have a problem with the boss or any of the employees, you may want to find a new job. Happy is what you want it to be. At least make sure it's comfortable.

Starting your own gig …

Maybe you can look into starting your own company or changing your career altogether. I know someone who started Look into different franchising or business opportunities but make sure to check out the current trends, so you are not investing in last year's money makers and this year's debt takers.

Ensuring that you can provide for our family is our number one goal, and we want to be able to do that as comfortable as possible. We must learn to adapt to where we are right now today in life. Work is our number one priority regardless of anything, i.e., race, gender, kind or like, etc. we are born to work to take care of ourselves and our families for the rest of our lives however long that may be, and these days they are getting longer.

Learn to be happy with the job that you have for someone somewhere does not have employment and may be hungry and or homeless as a result of that fact. We have to learn to create a happy spot in our heart and do what is necessary to have employment that is satisfying to our soul. If our soul cannot be sparked and kindled every day, we will not want to participate.

How sad of a life to have to live in a job that does not make you happy and when the alarm goes off you want to throw up. Yeah! It can take you there sometimes.

I wrote this article some years ago, about a producer of comedy, Walter Latham (Latham produced Kings and Queens of Comedy).

As I researched him on the internet about his life and his business, I became fascinated with one aspect of his success. I thought, "Walter Latham, we should be honored and privileged to have a promoter with such passion." What I learned was that Mr. Latham intrigued me deeply and here is why: He gave up what most people would die to achieve —Hollywood, the ultimate dream. To keep the visions alive and be able to help more comedians to achieve their place in the cosmic realm, he chose to create the type of family and work life that will allow him to be all that he can be. Who would pack up a Hollywood office in exchange for your client's success and happiness?

Walter Latham did just that in 2005 and had never lived to regret it. Making this decision helped create the perfect dynasty for Latham Entertainment. Latham Entertainment, based in Greensboro, NC, is the largest independently owned and operated comedy promotion-company in the country. Latham is currently working to bring more comedians to the big screens. Read the entire article at http://wp.me/pN12u-qr and visit his website Latham Entertainment: www.lathamentertainment.com.

Mr. Latham had to make a choice in his life to protect his family of comedians, clients, and his family by moving his company out of the money central (Hollywood) and move to a more stable and peaceful environment to be more productive. It's all about sacrificing your "now" for your future. https://www.youtube.com/user/LathamEntertainment http://walterlatham.com/

Doing What You Love

My friend Rosemary has a passion for literacy and children's education. She is a mother of a bookworm and an avid reader herself. As a stay-at-home, Rosemary spent a lot of her time reading books and adding to her child's book collection. One day Rosemary stumbled across a fabulous and fun work-from0home opportunity on the internet. Feeling the need to get out of the house, get back to work and get back into the real social world with child in tow, she thought, why not Join this publishing company and get paid to read and share these books with others?

So Rosemary decided to join Usborne & Kane Miller Publishing Co. as an independent Literacy Consultant. Now, she teaches literacy to kids in her community and shares the Love For Literacy for a Lifetime; Reading is a Gift Book Fairs, Toys for Tots, and more! Rosemary is making a positive difference in children's' lives with books & programs that Usborne offers. If you are a stay-at-home mom, you can make a difference I children's lives too.

If you would like information on how to become an Independent

Literacy Consultant with Usborne Books and More in your area, refer to their main website at www.UsborneBooksandMore.com or contact Rosemary by email at UsborneP3571@gmail.com.

There are so many ways that you can make a difference and do what you love. Choosing to leave a legacy for your family to follow like my friend Darwin Ali who started Leave A Legacy Scholarship Foundation.
Children can learn to start their college fund, so they are prepared for immediate expenses college may bring.
There are so many things you can do to help your family and your community of peoples.

I am so happy with the fact that I have choices in life that I can truly make the choice of which jobs to apply for or which clients to accept in my business. Take a look at your view master slide ... from the moment you open your eyes in the morning; you have a choice as to how your day will go down. Every day, you carry that choice of the freedom to choose.

And to be honest, your choice should always lead you to happiness no matter where you are in life.
Creating movies and bringing life stories to light like Mr. William Belcher. William is working on "Stick and Move" the movie (coming soon). He decided to follow something that he loves doing. Creating. If you can think it, belief, create it and you shall see it, come to life. Will has a few more movies that he is creating and loving every minute of it. Doing what he loves and he shall prosper at what he does.

I became a wedding planner, officiant, and a life coach because I love helping people. I wanted to be able to help people start their beautiful life together however they dreamed it and can afford it. It's also the reason I became an officiate as well. Being positive energy and love that unites the couple, not just someone with an empty heart and hidden money agendas. You should always strive to be a blessing or positive energy in what you do. You should love what you do and do what you love.

Some people love being parents, and some people love careers. Whatever it is you choose to do in life, choose to do it with love.

We can be anything we want in life ..we first have to believe in ourselves. We must first think it, believe in it, write it out, and then achieve it.

Remembering to ...

- Smile and be happy or make some changes in your career

- Choose employment that will make you happy and bring you joy

- Change your furniture around, add some accessories

- If you can, add some bright colors

- Don't allow what co-workers do affect your attitude

- Choose to think, before speaking

- Remember that at all times you are playing in the work game

- Keep your game piece shinned up and ready to make a move

- Positive mind thinking will help you get through the day

- Do stretches or small exercise when time allows

- Remember most importantly, to BREATHE!

Put an alarm on your phone if needed to remind you to breathe five times from the bottom of your stomach and the depth of your soul. When your breathing is right, everything can be right. It's all in your frame of mind and the air you breathe. The workplace is a perfect place to practice patience and kindness. Not everyone has control at home so they may take it out at the office.

Don't be afraid of these kinds of people. Happy is what happy does, and if you bring in some snacks for everyone or some donuts now and then, people will learn to be just as happy in the future. Life will be what we make it, even at the office.

NOTES:

9 Live, Love and Be Fabulous

Whether you're a man or a woman, you have all the right in the world to live your life the way you want it, love whom you wish to love and be as fabulous as you want to be...

I have a saying that keeps me focused; Forgive your past, Live in the present, and Embrace your future. You cannot change the past so forgive yourself for anything that is over and done with. If you need to apologize to someone, do so, but you have to forgive your past. You can't do anything about it. Living in the present means to live for today. Not going back and not trying to go forward. Today, is what we are living for? Embracing your future means to be prepared for what the future may bring. You should not try to alter the future in any way, live for today.

You don't have to have a lot of money to live your life fabulously. All it takes is a little time and talent, and you can have the fabulous life you deserve.

Now rewind... really! That sounds like a bunch of bull crap right? Right... well not really. It is what it is. If you want to live a fabulous life you can. Life is what you make it. Pull out your view master slide ... If you want to hang out at the theater, do so. If you want people to know you at the coffee shop, become a regular and talk to others. You have a choice as to how you live. You can do anything that you wish when your time and money allows you to.

That is what we should teach our children. When they go to college and get a degree, it enables them to be able to live as fabulous as the degree is going to let them. If they want to be on yachts every day, then they may want to become an engineer. You have to teach them what careers will pay them and what type of lifestyle that will entail.

They may have more of motivation if it is shown to them in their face that way.

You have to be able to create what you may want. Life is and will always be what you create it to be.

Even if you have limited funds, you can still have fun. I love going to the park, even if it's just to sit and read or write my stories. No real motive just some time to yourself and a great atmosphere. Head over to the beach if you have one. Take an umbrella and forget about the rest, just go and have fun. Make it fun for yourself. Invite someone or no one at all; it's your call. But know that it does not take someone else to ride with you for you to have fun and be happy. I spend most of my time out alone. I go to the mall and the movies alone. I shop alone and do so many things alone.

If you have to wait for someone else to be able to come with you, you may never make it to places that you want to go. Choices in our lives are for us to make based on how happy we want to be. From the moment you wake up in the morning ... you have a choice to be happy.

And from there the rest is history. Just because the world is pooping on you doesn't mean that you poop back. You pull out an umbrella, and you keep it moving. There will always be things and people that will try to rain poop on your parade.

You do not have to stand there and accept it. You have a choice, and sometimes loving people from a distance is your only choice. If something breaks the monotony of a peaceful and happy life than it must be removed, the family include.

You don't have to go out and kill anyone. What I am saying is that you can let your loser boyfriend/girlfriend know that you would like to separate or get a divorce. You can agree that just because you are sisters, doesn't mean that you are going to tolerate and accept the rude behavior. You can simply love or deal with people from a distance.

You don't have to go to their house, you don't have to call them, but you do have to respect them and be perfectly ok with being around them at family functions. Just learn the limits, and you will be ok. You know how much of your life to share with others.

Living your life the way you want will create some lonely times. Once you start eliminating the unnecessary people and things, you may end up feeling alone. Don't take it personally, you need to put your foot down and live your life for you and not others.

Living life, means to take the time out to do things for you. Take yourself out to lunch. Treat yourself to the movies. Buy yourself a new hat, or take a bubble bath instead of a shower. So many of us stopped taking baths; your body needs to be sometimes soaked. Your body needs to know that you care about its wellbeing.

Have you had a foot massage lately? You may be standing on the solution to all your ills. Your feet take the brunt of almost everything we do in life. How much time do you spend on your feet? We spend way too much time on our feet to not take care of them; your feet are like your car. You need an oil change and tune-up now and then or the car will not run properly.

The same goes for your body. You may need a tune up every couple of months. You may need to get a full body massage, neck and shoulder, and or feet. I see Sharon Carroll and Stan Elijah, for my body wellness needs. They are both great masseuses who come to the rescue. They even make house calls. While you are at it, visit your local chiropractor office. They can help you with all sorts of ills, i.e., allergy, asthma, high blood pressure, penile dysfunction as well as fertility. Your nerves for everything you need to survive are located at the spine, therefore, treating the spine gently treats the issues that may be accruing.

Some things that are wrong with us may be about age, but mostly due to the age of the problem that was never taken care of so now it's a major issue after so many years of unintentional neglect. I have a special chiropractor (Dr. Jeanette Reed) who specializes in Subluxation which is a total lifesaving specialty. With a few car accidents under my belt, she was able to make me functional again as well as get me off of my lifetime asthma medication (it's been about four years asthma and medication free). She treated my spine for my back and neck injury, and in the process of treating the whole spine, she was able to treat those specific nerves altogether.

It's a total win-win for me. I can't ever remember a time when I didn't have to own an inhaler. Dr. Jeanette "Jet" Reed D.C. (now in Denver, Colorado) was able to help me get a piece of my life back by caring about her career and her patients by loving what she does and helping to heal people with her special gifts and talents. She believes her reward comes when seeing her patients walk again or something simple like breathing. I see her as my angel for without her; I had no hope. My recovery process is far from over, but I am at the point of having hope for with proper future treatment ...I can be healed and without the need for surgery or medication.

Your body deserves it, and so do you. Once you take care of your body, your body will, in turn, take care of you.

Love can come in many forms. It does not always mean that you have to be in love with a person. It can also mean, loving yourself or your family. Whatever it is, love is essential to living. You need to love to prosper. It's a part of growing. Love for those who have spouses should be taken to next levels. Add some variety to your life. Take some weekend trips. Find each other all over again. Did you know since you have been married or together that each of you has developed a whole new liking to some stuff? There are so many new things that you all developed over the course of the relationship and now is a good time to know each other all over again.

Go out on some dates. Make sure to schedule them so that there are no excuses. While being spontaneous is fun and exciting, just make sure that you commit to at least two dates a month. Of course, it will depend on how much real time you have between you two and the lives that you live. Once you start doing this, you will love it so much you will want more.

Being married or together with someone can also mean that sex times are off balance. One thing you have to realize is that when adults have family and jobs, life can be overwhelming and tiring and sex just falls short. I would rather get into my bed to sleep at the end of the day because I am exhauststed versus wanting to be romantic and having bedtime rendezvous. Let's face it, once you hit that bed, it's over.

So what do you do? Try having sex during the early evening time. Slap that man on the butt right after or even before dinner. Try to get some kissing time in over the pot of spaghetti. You can even make dinner, have the kids sit down to eat alone (if they are old enough) and go make out in the back seat of the car. Eat when you get back inside, make it fun.

Or how about you wake up at my favorite hour of five o'clock in the morning? That is the best time in the world to have sex. You have rested well, and your body is nice and warm and receptive to feeling sexual. I feel most of my sexuality at this hour of the morning.

There has to be compromising for any and all of this to work. When one plan does not work, simply set it on fire (not literally) and start over. You have to understand that not everything we want to do in life will work out with the people in it. You have to be willing to reschedule, change or cancel the date or project altogether. Life is about adapting to the situation at hand. So do not fall apart when the romantic dinner and rose pedals go unnoticed because your spouse had to work late or the sitter called at the last minute and canceled. If those things happen, take your spouse's dinner to work and put rose petals in his or her pocket. Include the kids at the candlelit dinner.

The kids may love it, and you are teaching them that families can do this together.

There are so many ways that you and your family can live a fabulous life. Your new attitude is fabulous within itself. How nice are you now? Isn't it a great feeling to wake up and you have a choice whether or not to be happy today? And you choose 'yes' to happiness...

People accidentally take life for granted. Forget that you have choices in life. Forget that you can change. Well, start now, it's not too late.

You can never be too late for change; it's what we live for. Trying to rediscover who you are can also be a scary thing. But with love, patience and time, everything is possible. Just try it and see if you have not already.

Remembering to ...

- Live, love and be as fabulous as you want to be

- Live life for you while respecting others

- Love each day as a new day

- Love yourself first

- Be as fabulous as your funds allow

- Do not create new debt being fabulous

- Being fabulous dwells in actions as well as things

- Create your own fabulous

- Share love with others daily

You have a right to live as fabulous as your funds allow you to without creating a debt of any kind. Life was given to us to work, live and be happy. If we are not happy, how do we expect to live? You only have control of you, and you must create the wonderful that you look for in your everyday life. Don't wait for someone else to create your fabulousness!

NOTES:

10 Accepting Who We Are As People

It was really hard to start living for me and accepting who I was at that time in my life. I had to work hard at creating a new life for myself. Not everyone likes it but I love it and the way I see it, it's our lives, and we should be living it the way we want to for at least this moment.

We have done a great job at caring for the need of others and will continue to. We're just adding some much needed "me time" to the plate. I can't tell you how your life will end up, whether your married single or divorced, the bottom line is accepting you for you as well as the "others" around you. Everyone has a right to be who they are, but you do not have to allow it in your circle. I cannot stress it enough. You have choices as to how you live your life and with whom you allow in it.

You see, there is a circle around you that allows your peace, air, sanity, and well-being. If you allow too many people or the wrong type of people in your circle, the circle will eventually swallow you whole while the rest of them continue with life and you will no longer exist.

Circle of Life ...

You have to accept the fact that the new you will create some lonely days, fun days, sad days, glad days, and any other days you and you alone will create. They will be what you allow it to be, what you create it to be. What will today bring? What will you create for yourself today?

My girlfriend and I were out shopping one day and while we were walking down the aisle of the store…well, at least I thought I was walking (*lol*)…my girlfriend stopped me by touching my arm, looked at me funny and said, "Are you skipping?" That was just funny to hear someone say!

90

I have a passion for life, one that I created for myself and I have to find a way to enjoy the things we are forced into doing. I don't know why I walk on my toes and skip when I walk, but it tells me and shows me in my view master slide that there is contentment in my life.

Hmm...that speaks volumes. Contentment for whom and what I am right now. Not what I have or how much of it I have, but who I am today. I cannot change who I was born to be. That was created for me, but I can change how I raise myself once the reigns are passed over. I am the only person or thing that has control over me. You are the only person that has control over you and only you. Are we using that control to our ability? Are we creating our lives how we want it to be lived? Or, are we simply just living and saying, "Oh well!"?

What would you do differently? Again, write it down and make it happen. Why would you wait any longer to enhance your life? Working on a better relationship, marriage, work, etc. is important, but working on you is even more important. If you don't take care of you ... well, who will?

There may not be any hands raised when you ask that question out loud so don't be alarmed. Creating your life for you and who you need to be for you is your mission. If you are not happy with you then who will be? No one! Let's not live a life that way. Let's live life as fabulous as we can, and that doesn't mean extravagant, it just means happy! We have to live this life anyway, so why not just be happy with who and what we are today?

Maybe having children is not for you. Don't have them if you feel you don't want them. BE REAL ABOUT IT! It's your life and not the life of others. You have to be comfortable with who and what you are. Maybe being single is not what you want and you may want to venture out and start looking for a husband or wife. We know that this may take some time, so you must be patient and open to different suggestion and variety. Change is always good and always expected. Change in any form can be good or bad depending on your motivation. Make one small change at a time. If you were to look in the mirror, would you be happy with who you are? Do you accept the person that you see or are you open to the possibilities of change?

Sometimes we cannot help how people view us or what aura we seem to give out, but we can accept ourselves and others for who and what we are today. We cannot change our skin color, our parents, and family but we can change our view of life.

If you don't like your hair color, well change it. If you do not like your clothing, well, you can change that as well. If you don't like your attitude, by all means, feel free to change it. If there is more than one thing about you that you do not like, start with one and go from there. Once you change one thing, the rest is easy.

Being in the purgatory of life doesn't have to be the end of you or your marriage or relationship. I cannot stress it enough... life will always be what you make it...point blank...period!

As I am writing this chapter, I chose to drive over to the park on this beautiful day and write. I wanted to enjoy the sun, smell the grass and flowers and watch the children play as I ponder about life and what will become of every one of us.

As I sit here, I'm watching an old man in his 70's or early 80's jogging around the park. I'm assuming he chose to make a difference in his life. He chose to not sit at home and complain about how old he is, and he got up, got out and is building a better heart and a better life for himself! If only for one more day.

People are playing soccer with big smiles on their faces and over by the swings are little children running and throwing a ball … laughing together.

Thinking about another type of scenario, they could be indoors getting on each other's nerves; but they chose to come outside and enjoy the day for what it was. Again, if only for one more day.

There are many people from different walks of life, different ways of living but the common trait that we all share should and always be the pursuit of happiness. Not the acquirement of things but the general fact of just being happy. You don't have to work like a slave to acquire things and people to be happy. Whatever you choose to do to acquire it should be something you love, and with that, you will always love yourself.

How many of us make it a point to be kind to others, to be happy every day? Not many will, but all will complain about not being happy at some point. Whoever you are, there you will always be! You cannot change who you are, but you can change who you chose to be only if you are not already happy. Sure you may be happy but think about it … you can always use a little more sunshine and happy days. Happy is what happy does! You have to create the happy; the happy doesn't create you!

No one is responsible for making sure you have a smile on your face. It is all up to you to make that happen. You are the only person or thing you have control over. No one else is allowed that control.

It's not anyone else job to blow sunshine up your butt!

Here comes an old lady riding her bike, she's about 78 or 80 years old. Just peddling along her way with a smile on her face like she doesn't have a care in the world, what an inspiration to see, choosing to ride her bike instead of staying indoors watching a television show that is on repeat for the 400th time. She is happy to be who she is at this moment in her life. It shows in her actions and her smile. I want to be like her when I grow up.

When you are creating a happier you, you may find resentment from others around you whether at home, work, church or school. Don't worry about the feelings of others as long as you are not purposely giving them a reason to dislike you. If you are simply living your life and being happy, then no one has a right to resent or dislike you but because it is a free world ... go for it!

You only have control of you and keep being the happiest you can be. You do not have to seek the approval of others to be it. It's a part of being the happy you, ignoring the negative and accepting the positive. You should never feed into any form of drama in life. It's part of the unnecessary that we spoke about earlier. Just be happy being you and others will follow. Either they will follow, or they will leave you the heck alone because who has time for anything but happiness.

The happy me is one who decided to be happy with who and what I am right now today. Not who I use to be, not who I want to be but who I am today. That means the person that you are right now as you are reading this. If you choose to be happy you will be happy. Take off the frown and put on a crown. Act like the prince or princess you were made to be!

The happy me has found a job that makes me happy. With a job that makes you happy you are looking forward to going to work, you are ok with waking up early and put forth great efforts to get your job done. The happy me has purchased some plants to take care of.

"Why?" you may ask. Well ...to learn how to care for someone or something other than myself if not forced to! In this quest, I will learn if I want to take care of plants, fish or dogs or if I simply just like doing it alone. If we don't try new and different things, we will never know where our satisfaction will come. I'm sorry, but I don't want to feed a plant every day, I just don't see the pleasure in that. But that's just my life and has nothing to do with yours.

I love plants and gardens but I know that I am no good at keeping them alive so why would I venture into something that would make my day worse than it already is. Learning who you are and what you like is all about taking chances and trying new things.

The happy me decided to go out and dance at least once a month; this gives me the opportunity to be around grown-ups, let my hair down and meet new people. It gives me an opportunity just to be me. I can go with friends or alone, I don't have a problem, either way, I enjoy the night, and all is well. If you can create a happy spot what would it be? What would make you happy right now at this moment with who you are and what you have?

When you think about what will make us happy, we have to be realistic. Being realistic is not saying having a million dollars will make me happy right now because how will you get that right now? It will not just fall out the sky so, be more realistic. Sitting in a hot tub right now would make me happy … I don't know about you, but that should make anyone happy. And throw in a 2-hour massage!

Being happy with who and what you are right now today is not an easy task, but you have to make it happen every day. Sure it takes a conscious effort to smile and say hello to someone, but once you start, you will find that you enjoy doing it regardless of the response.

Being happy with you will always be determined by how happy you want to be and how much effort you will put into it. Everything you do in life requires an effort. Stop giving up on things because you have to put a little work into it. I know you want a break from time to time, but life does not always allow it, so keep it moving.

Remembering to ...

- Accept the person you were created to be

- Live for today and today only

- Remember you have only control over yourself

- You have no control what family you were born into

- Use your control of your actions to help others

- Sometimes days will be lonely and sad but take the control and change it

- Consider if having children is the best thing for you ... at least right now in your life

- Understand, not everyone will have children

- Hold people accountable for the way they treat you

- Go out to the park and sit and people watch

- Appreciate life as it is and learn how to upgrade your daily

You have to accept who you are. If you don't like or appreciate who you are, by all means, change it for the better. We want you to be happy, and sometimes that requires change. People may not like you, but I love you and so does a lot of other people, you just may not feel it.

We don't often feel love or kindness, but it exists ... somewhere. Remember, rejection is not always a bad thing. We were not meant to be inducted into everything and around everyone. Accept who you are, and the rest will either follow or leave. Either way, it's a benefit to you.

NOTES:

11 The Struggle

How many of us live without the struggle of life? No matter how old or what year it is, there will always be ...THE STRUGGLE!

Since we have to go through the struggle regardless of choice, we must ensure that our attitude is in the proper order to be able to handle the situations at hand. It's not what you go through its how you go through it that determines your outcome!

Again, life is what we make it, every day ... if we make it a struggle than a struggle it shall be.

Let's take our mindset to a different level for once we know better we are supposed to do better. If you are short on money for a bill how about evaluating which bill can be mailed out at this time.

There may be something that you can do without so that next month the struggle won't be as hard. Try cutting the cable bill and watching DVD's instead, you are always flipping through the remote anyway so let's just keep it moving.

By accepting the fact that this month may be a little harder than the others, my mind can have a little more peace. Changing our mindset about things will create a happier outcome.

Sure you may wish you can see your favorite program, but that's just temporary. Smile at the fact that you still live and it can help you to change your outlook on life. I'm just happy to own a television, and I can watch movies on my DVD player... See, happy!

The struggle to find a job can be overwhelming. How do you fix your mind not to be able to feed your family? The new homeless are people like you and I. We are the new social service recipients that some of us used to talk about over the years.

Making it by on a wing and a prayer, the struggle can be just about anything from a bad conversation with your mother to the fight with your best friend that was as trivial as pre-school fun. Grow up and get over some stuff so you can live, if even just a little. Learn to be the better person in all your relationships, the better listener, the better friend, lover, mother, father, be the better of everything and everyone in your circle.

The struggle does not have to exist, or if they do, they don't have to be so monstrous. Let's learn to move on to some things.

The struggle today is a little different than it was years ago. The world today has become so full of people and things that our minds are not used to having less, being told no or making the sacrifice. You see, we are accustoming to having any and everything that we want whenever we want it. We have entirely too much stuff with the need and desire for more. This can often cause a struggle within itself.

Having two car notes and insurance can be a lot of work mentally and physically when your family is barely making it. It has now become a struggle to go to work every day because all that is on your mind is paying those two car notes and insurance which doesn't even fall in with the rest of the bills and issues.

It's now your main focus that you worry about every day. What if you are ill and cannot make it work? You will not be paid for the day(s) off, and the rent has to be paid so what do you do?

How do you go through the struggle? Do you find a solution that makes sense and easy to accomplish? Maybe purchase a car that is paid in full at tax time or sell the one you have and use the extra money to buy one that you can pay in full. There may be a solution you can come up with that would relieve the struggle.

There should be things we go through in life that is not so complex. Finding solutions is not always the answer, but one thing that is certain is…if you have the right frame of mind, you can make it through any struggle presented to you.

Make wonderful regardless if the world seems to be pooping all over you ... you are not supposed to poop back!

Do you even evaluate why you are struggling? Write it down and evaluate the situation. See how and when you can change or eliminate something or someone.

There is always a benefit to writing things down so you can see more clearly as if looking in the window from the outside. Everyone around you can see it except you... but if you write it down and evaluate it... you can see it too!

Is there a struggle to make it work every day? Sometimes the car is acting up, or you may not have a car altogether and getting to work becomes a daunting task. Is there a struggle to get along with the people at work? Often a combination of attitudes can clash at any given moment. Everyone will not get along regardless of the mission. But we can change our mindset to adapt to what we need to adapt to, to get through the day. We become the lead actor/actress in our play. Work it out the best you can until you can find a new job or a new car. Be happy that you have the job, for without it you will not be able to live. Looking at things a little more different can help a little. It is hard to determine when to lose it in your mind but just knows that if you do lose your mind, there is always the lost and found ... you can come in and find your mind anytime you are ready. It's up to you when that time is.

We have a right to be angry, hurt, confused, happy, sad, and joyous or whatever feeling that we may have at the time. We don't have to allow negative energy to fester in our lives. We do not have to stay angry. We can be angry, say what we need to say, do what we need to do and keep it moving. Keeping it moving is very important. If you are angry today, do not carry that into tomorrow. Analyze the situation and see what can be done if anything and let it go.

We have to remember that we create our happiness, sadness or whatever feeling we encore. If you received sadness, make it for a short time so that you are not weighed down with it. Carrying sadness can keep you from prospering. Keep you from living. The struggle again will come, but how do you create your outcome? Are you contributing to the struggle or does the struggle seem just to find you?

There are always solutions if you look hard enough. For the most part, we are only in control of ourselves. We have the control to see what our role is in every situation that we are in. What role are you playing in your struggle? Are you the author, creator or bystander? Once you write it down and evaluate it, let me know. I would love to know what role you played.

Sometimes we can sabotage's our own lives. We have a desire to succeed but may not know how to handle the success, so we don't allow the success even to take place. Get comfortable with having less, so the stress of wanting more doesn't overtake you.

We struggle with our minds on a regular basis. It seems to be a constant battle to do right. There is a constant struggle to turn the other cheek, and if I have to keep my mouth shut one more time when someone says something offensive, I will just scream.

Always a struggle but your reactions will create your outcome... Don't be on the defense. If someone accuses you then simply provide the proof with a smile. If you are cut off on the road, simply throw a smile and say, "Have a great day!" Want to park up front at the store today, ask for a favor before you leave the house. There are always things that we can do to help contribute to a better day than simply allowing things to happen. We can help detour things a bit, per say.

Children struggle to fit in but may not be taught how to fit in. There can be things that can be taught to help with the struggle if an adult is willing to help out. Children struggle to like what they are expected to like without allowing them their mind and desires. There are so many struggles that children go through that are unnecessary when we take the time to actually raise them instead of allowing the world to raise them.

You may be struggling with your parents as they get older. We are supposed to ensure that as they get older, we help them to make decisions regarding their retirement that will be as gentle as possible. Taking on elder children, per say, is a lot of work and if not planned properly you can be overwhelmed with old children just when yours may be leaving the nest.

Some talks should take place and perhaps a long-term care insurance plan secured in the younger years to ensure the transition is an easier one than not.

Some things can be done ahead of time if only everyone would talk about it and put it in writing. There may not always be enough time to do things as things do happen, but at least you can prepare as much as possible ahead of time so that you are not in an unnecessary struggle.

Remember to be aware of your role in the things that occur in your life. We are responsible for everything. People only do to you what you allow them to do. If you cannot accept that fact, then you might want to stay away from people. Whatever you can do to eliminate your struggle will be a benefit to you and everyone around you.

There are struggles within the home with family and/or friends. There is the husband or wife that you can't seem to please, the children that may not obey or the bills that keep coming without the money to cover them. Attitude is everything. How are you speaking when you speak? How is your body language?

Personally, I remember my ex would just cringe his face when he was angry or frustrated about something. He would not even have to say anything, for his face would say it all and put me into defense mode causing an immediate reaction that was not good.

If he had changed the face when he was put in the position, it would have created a better outcome for our conversations. You can try not to let things bother you, but the reality is that they do bother you but let's just get through it.

So knowing this, I tried not to allow his facial expression to piss me off. It didn't work at all, and I was always pissed at his facial expression. As a gesture, I would learn to quickly look the other way even if I had to put my hand on my face so I couldn't see his facial expression when it happened. I tried my best to come up with a solution that would help the both of us. Sometimes distance is all that will help. You have to determine that for yourself.

We should be taking one day at a time. There is enough stuff in today to think about without having to stir up tomorrow's dishes. One day at a time or small time frames to help you make it through today.

Before starting tomorrow, how about evaluating today? What was great today and why? What was not so great and why? What could I have done differently? What role did I play in the outcome?

Once you make those determinations, you can better navigate through the next one. I surely learned a lot about my role in all this. The lessons must be learned, so we do not repeat the struggle. Without learning the lesson, we will not only repeat the struggle but get through it with more difficulty next time.

Struggling is our second nature. Sin is our first. When we didn't like the way we walked, we changed it to be more appealing. When our eyes could no longer see, we bought glasses. When we want a nice car to drive, we figure out a way to secure it.

I have a friend who is a dream dealer ... Demetrius Walls. He works for Mercedes in Sacramento, California (you never know where he is right now lol his locations changes) and can help you make your dreams come true. On his social media page, he usually posts pictures of himself with the beautiful people who have chosen to make their dreams a reality. What I see are the happiest people within those photos. The energy that is in their smile and face is the energy of satisfaction and relief from the everyday mundane way. They have chosen to upgrade their lives by purchasing a happy drive. I don't call Demetrius a salesman; for a salesman has to create a sale. He is a miracle to other people because he helps them not just purchase a vehicle, but to make sure it's affordable and reliable.

With his honesty and integrity, he will help you choose what is best for you and your family.

He is never in it for the actual sale (but of course we should be paid for our time) but he loves what he does, and it shows in how much he cares for his clients or family of friends as he calls them. And it doesn't hurt that he's funny as all outdoors... makes you want to throw him in the trunk of your new ride and take him home with you (laughing). It's hard to find good honest people so make sure when choosing a large investment as a family vehicle that you have someone you can rely on and trust. Often, people think they cannot afford such luxury when in reality almost everyone can! Let Demetrius help you to secure your HAPPY! Can you smell it? Oooh! I just love a new car smell!

Life is what we make it. We have choices in our own lives. We use those choices how we see fit. We do what we want to do when we want to do it so why are we not making wonderful in everything we do so that we can live a prosperous and happy life? Why do we get a job that is too far for us to commute? Why do we hire a babysitter we can tell will not do the job right? Why do we smoke when we know it may cause us cancer? Again, what role are we playing?...

Signing up for adult boot camp should be an option for some of us. If you were unaware, everything in life must be learned. If you are not willing to be taught by someone, how will you know how to go through it? Did you see someone else handle the same situation? Did you read it in a magazine or book or did you listen to the adults in your life when they were trying to school you on different subjects?

Adult boot camp may be able to teach us a few things about courtesy or forgiveness. It may teach us how to hug one another and to say thank you or please. Adult boot camp may be able to help us make it through the struggles in life as well as the joys. You see, once you learn the secrets to living; you can create joy instead of struggles. Struggles will become things that just happen instead of things that cause problems.

I use to struggle to get up in the morning. I hated getting out of bed in the cold or the heat or whatever the reason was getting up in the morning was not exciting.

One day I decided that I had to change my mindset on the subject. What would make me feel better about getting up in the morning? Once I started getting up and paying attention to the things I did and wanted to do, I was able to put a plan together.

Once I woke up in the morning, I would turn on my music and get my mind dancing. I decided I needed to do things that were pleasing to my mind. I listened to music and discovered the morning was a perfect time to write my stories or do my work of any kind. I love mornings now! I can get more done by 10 a.m. than most people do all day.

Changing the way I thought about mornings helped me to become the author that I am today. It helped me to become the creator that God instilled in me. If only I had changed my mindset sooner, I thought. But know that everything come in due time!

"Everything that you are capable of being is already inside of you. It's up to you to be still enough to allow your gifts and talents to manifest. In due time, all things can come to light." Summer B

Remembering to …

- Know there will always be a struggle, keep your mind right
- If your mind is right, you can make it through anything
- Life will be what we make it, every day
- Plan for a rainy day
- Look at the people in your life and choose accordingly
- Make things a little easier on yourself by eliminating unnecessary things
- Make wonderful regardless of what the world dishes out
- Be happy with what you have and who you are
- Write down your weekly plan of life to help relieve stress
- Secure your senior years, so you are not a burden to your children
- Don't allow others to rain on your parade
- Have as many parades as you want to have, in your honor

NOTES:

12 Recovering What Was Lost

Why would you want to recover a piece of what was lost? Apparently, you didn't want it, or you would not have lost it and taken better care of it. What did you lose anyway? Is it a lost dog, cat, hair or happiness? What exactly did you lose and how do you think we can get it back?

Happiness — if you lost happiness. Well, I might be able to help you find that again or for the first time; whatever your story is. Finding your happy spot can sometimes be a little easier than you thought. Sometimes it's a matter of stepping out of your box or getting rid of your box altogether.

If you can recover the good old days, let me know **how**, so I can join you. Other than that, there is no recovering what was lost. For yesterday no longer exists. You only get one chance at today and tomorrow is not guaranteed, so whatever it is you need to do or say, do or say it today! Again… we don't have rollover minutes, and I have things to do so let's keep life moving in a positive direction.

The recovery department is full of requests and it amazes me what the answers are as to why you want to recover what you want to recover …

NAME	ITEM LOST	REASON FOR RECOVERY
Pearl	Boyfriend Tom	At least he was around, and I won't be lonely.
Alex	Cowboy Collection	Miss the space being crowded. It's lonely.
Trina	Date Nights	Feel lonely inside. Want to hang out.

Well, often times we don't need to recover items of the past. We should be moving on to bigger and much better things at all times. Sure you may have the ability to recover some old things, but why?

Take the opportunity to enhance yourself with other options. There is not always need to be in a comfort zone. That is most often the case when it comes to change. The comfort of knowing the outcome in advance, the comfort of knowing your role already without it being new and a learned experience.

You may want to recover a smile which is fine but the way you smile today versus twenty years ago will be the key that you will see is the difference in upgrading. Know that your smile will be larger and more meaningful for you have transitioned to a kinder spirit. There is no need to recover anything but respect for respect will always be your way through anything in life.

After I started my changes and transitions in my own life, I thought I wanted to be like the old me. The cute sexy, single, most wanted (so they said) woman I use to be (which I hated being) but for me, it was all I knew how to be. I had to learn how to be a new me with more enhancing features of life than before. Had I not realized that I couldn't be the person I use to be I could have gotten lost for longer than need be. Sometimes all it takes is for someone to share with you or for you to again, write it out so you can see for yourself where you can make some small changes which in the end will save your life.

We can be lost for a few months or many years but whatever the length of time you can make a comeback if you want to. You indeed have to want it, and it doesn't take a whole lot to do so.

Recovering your happiness is the key to everything here and once you can understand that happiness is the goal and mission we can work anything out. Someone curses you, smile and say have a good day… you can curse under your breath or pray for them, your choice but you just made an ugly situation a nicer one and believed you me that everyone was watching you and paying attention and when you walked away, they thought about that whole situation and said to themselves or others to hear that they don't know if they could have been as nice! And you know that's the whole truth. We have to be leaders in our communities which means, yes we do have to turn the other cheek on a regular basis.

Recovering the joy of life is a great mindset to have. Remembering a time when life was so great you would want to live it again. Remember, you are only looking for the smile and tingle that the thought of the memory brings, you don't want to relive it.

When I am going through things in life, and sometimes I just want to cry, I click my heels three times and the place I want to go back home to was in my younger days with all my friends in Laurel Park, and life was great. We all have a place we can remember good or bad but while remembering those times make sure it's beneficial to remember and if not, well, tuck it away and replace it with new and greater thoughts and memories. Life is what we will make it, and we must be making new memories every day.

Look at your view master and see all the things and people you lost along the way. You lost the desire to go outside and have fun.

All you do is sit around and watch TV or play video games all day and waste all that time feeling sorry for yourself or like being stuck on a couch or bed wasting time. How much time are you spending on social media when you can be researching and learning new things? There is a reality that does say, if you do something all the time over a long period, it may be time to change. It's like being stuck in a time, where you don't know how to dress anymore. You wear the same clothes you had twenty years ago and because it still fits you don't understand why you need to buy more. You like it so why should anyone have anything to say about it!

Get Your Mind Right …

After all is said and done, you should be on your way to a better you. The key to everything is getting your mind right for each situation and your transition of life. There will always be things, people, and situations that create the unnecessary but if you have your mind right, you can go through it with a much better outcome. It's not **what** you go through, its **how** you go through it.

You have to go through things in life anyway; so why not with the right preparation? If you know the kids need lunches for school tomorrow, well let's get them made today or tonight, so we have a little extra time to breathe. Keeping your mind right is another thing. Once you get your mind right, you must keep it together at all times. One must never get caught slipping.

You set the standards as to how you are going to live starting in high school and your choice of college or no college. Getting your mind prepared for life will be to know how much money you wish to make in life and what kind of job you would need to obtain that kind of money. Once you know what kind of job, you then need to know what is required and how to go about getting the education or experience to obtain the job or career. It's all about preparation and getting your mind right for the next move in your life.

The next step should already be thought of and ready to implement as each day approaches. The more prepared we are, the less stress we will have and the more happiness we will obtain. Getting your mind right is essential to living a better life and becoming a better you.

Recovering happiness with no regrets is a goal we all wish to obtain, right now today. In your 'right now, today' what would you change? What is it you would do differently? If you can change anything at all why would you change it? Is it something that would make you truly happy? Is it something that would benefit you in the long run or again, is it that tingly feeling of joy that you get when you think about it? Now that right there is something to consider really… is it the feeling that you get when you think about it?

Sometimes it's just better to start over. You know, like when you look at the box in the garage of papers and stuff that you need to go through, what if you just threw the box in the garbage without going through it? It was in the garage for six years now, if you haven't needed what was in it all that time, why now? If you didn't go through it, you actually would never know what you missed.

I have a friend who was producing comedy shows. (So many people are into laughter for it's a key to living well) Well after a while he started getting a little bored with that and decided to write a movie. He used his talents and his mind to put a real-life story together. Something in his mind was coming together because the comedy allowed him some of that inner peace. Once you establish inner piece, so many things in your mind are allowed to develop.
Things were always there in your mind, but you are always so busy that it takes longer to make a debut. For some, it may never.

This movie has not been produced as yet, but it's on its way. Progress and patience and perseverance. Staying true to oneself and keeping oneself aligned is essential. And my friend is very patient and in the meantime continues to do other things that he loves to do. You don't just stop there; you keep developing until there is nothing left to develop within yourself.
Prayerfully we will see the movie soon. Stick and Movie, the movie, already is ringing a bell in my head. Love the title and the story, can't wait to see it.

Remembering to ...

- Not dread in the past, you cannot change it

- Create new friends in your current new life

- Create new happiness in your everyday living

- Keep your mind right

- Making small changes as a regular upgrade

- Make a list of things you need to make you happy

- Make a list of things that do not currently make you happy

- Eliminate things that do not enhance your new life

You have to remember that your past is your past; you cannot change it or bring it back. You can only live for your today. Often we want the feeling of something that was lost and not the actual thing. We can reflect on the memory of it, but learn to create new memories for our future. You don't want to resurrect anything from your past. What you want is... to evaluate everything in your today to see if it fits in your future of tomorrow.

NOTES:

13 Don't Take It Personal

If you never learn anything else in life, make sure to learn this … you are the only person or thing that you have control over. You do not have authority over anyone else or thing.

Now that you understand that, you will be able to live with more peace of mind. I will share with you a few examples as to why you should not take it personally when things are out of your control.

The cashier at the local store shorts your change. Do you get upset and go off or do you simply point it out and settle it calmly? See, you have no control over what happened, but you do have control over how you react to what happened because you only have control over you. If you want you can add to the situation by creating a scene or something of that nature but as you know in life, things just aren't perfect, and there will always be situations that arise that may not be pleasing to us but we must learn to deal with them as they come with all the respect it deserves.

If your ex-husband or wife didn't pay the child support and you are tired of going through it … what do you do? Do you go off, and cut off contact with the child and parent? Or do you realize that you have control over your reaction and the proper way to react is to calmly understand that you have no control over any of that and you have to move forward the best way you can until it is resolved or settled?

Knowing that you have no control over other people or things will help you deal with your life a little easier … Think of all the time you save not worrying about things because it's not in your control to do so. You can let some things go altogether because some things just are not worth your time or efforts when they have to be settled by other people.

Free your mind!

If people do not accept you for who you are, don't take it personally. It's not your job to monitor people's fires and desires. Everyone isn't supposed to like or approve of everyone or thing. It's ok if people do not like the way you dress or if people don't like the fact that you lost weight. We don't have time to worry about those people, we have a life to live and that life has nothing to do with anyone else but you.

It can revolve around someone else's life, but your life is all about you and what you need and want. We have to make sure that when you are living a life with your family that you do include yourself as well. Don't feel guilty taking time out for you, or buying something for yourself. If you do not treat yourself special, how will you teach others to treat you? They often follow by example so be careful shorting yourself in life!

People will want to be your friend no longer or sit next to you on the bus. There will be all sorts of things that will come up with the new you, but you cannot take it personally. You may feel lonely and afraid because you may be more alone than usual but that's ok … that's the time you are supposed to use to learn about you and who you are and what you like in life. The less time you will be spending on drama, and the issues drama bring that more time you will have to do what makes you happy.

Trust me when I say it may feel easier to go back to your old ways so you can have more friends and more things to do but look at all the drama you went through when you were in those friendships or partnerships etc. There are just some things in life that's worth sacrificing for, and a peace of mind is one of them. That alone time gets a little easier if that's the case but remember; you can always find and create new family and friends. When you create your new you that meant that you would be doing new things in your life that will enable you to meet new people. You can choose to be friends or simply in passing.

When people stop inviting you places or asking for your advice, don't take that personal. That does not mean that they don't value your opinion that simply means, at that moment they didn't ask you. It may or may not have anything to do with you, but that's ok because they have a right to seek opinions from anyone they chose as do you.

If you didn't get the phone call first that your sister was pregnant, well, so what you were not first on the list. How old are we that we are holding people accountable for not making you number one!

When someone picks up the phone for the first time to tell important news, there is only one phone number they can dial unless they do a conference call. One phone number is all they can dial, and you are upset and having a hissy fit because you were not the one phone number on this particular day. Ok … Think it and get it over it! And get over it fast because you are too old to be tripping over small and trivial things.

You only have control over yourself, so you know that you were not the one making the phone calls to tell the news, so you have to deal with how it happened, like it or not. When it's your turn to deliver the news or something else in life, make sure you do it how it's supposed to be done as well. You only have control over the things you say and the things you do.

Learn to laugh instead of anger. If you learn to think the "no control" part and look at who you are dealing with, just laugh. Laugh at the fact that life happens and things will always happen. You can always learn something from every situation that you go through. If you can learn the lessons as you go along, you won't have to relive them again.

A lesson from the child support situation could be; missing the payment made me realize that I need to save more of my money so in the event my ex-does not pay on time again, my son will have what he needs.

There are lessons in everything we do in life … take the time to sit back and think about some things before reacting to them, and you will find easier solutions than the ones you were going to rush into. You cannot control other people's actions, but you sure can control your reaction. Your reaction is essential to how the rest plays out. Hmm…that says a mouthful right there. Your reaction regardless of the situation that was given you will determine the outcome.

How well are your reactions? How would your family and friends say you handle reactions? Will they say you are nuts or will they say that you handle them calmly and well mannered?

I cannot stress it enough that you cannot take life so personally. It's not for you to take on with such a short lifespan.

Your actions and reactions will create your life. You are the one controlling your actions and reactions to life. Are you doing a good job or can you use some help? Sometimes you have to ask yourself that question … Its ok if you can use a little help you know. People get help for all sorts of things and if you don't really know how to live your life then, by all means, get some help in the areas you need and never feel less than for doing so.

Life does not come with a book and if you do not have the proper teachers in life (home as well as school) then you will not know how to live in a grown-up world and will simply be moving about as you see. If you did not get the job you wanted, you should not always take that personal. Sometimes we want something that we are not supposed to have, or there was a more qualified person to get the job, and it just wasn't you. You cannot take that personal, for you only have control over you, and you, unfortunately, are not the interviewer or hirer.

It's their loss for not hiring you if you do not get the job and who knows, maybe now you are open for the other job that you are supposed to have.

Ok so you are looking in the mirror and wondering why you didn't get the job, the girl, the husband, the children, the car and you are wishing you were different ... wishing you were whatever was needed to get what you wanted. There will always be something in life that will make you wonder, wish or want but you have to know that life is only what you make it and what's under your control. You cannot control your female organs, you cannot give yourself the job, and you cannot make the woman or man want to be your spouse.

Only you have control over your actions and reactions. If you did not wear the right clothing to the job interview that caused them not to give you the job then that's a different story. But if you did everything right on your part (what you had control of) then you are free to have a peace of mind with the outcome whether it was what you wanted or not.

If you want to be happy and others around you don't want to be happy, what do you do? Do you join their sorry party or do you make wonderful anyway? We are accountable for what we do, right or wrong you know. If you join the sorry party do you not know that your life will become that way and next thing you know, you will be the leader of the sorry group. If you want to be happy and others do not want to be happy you are to be happy anyway. Why are allowing others to rain on your parade?

That's like you having eyes and allowing someone to take them because they don't want you to see. Let sorry people be sorry people for themselves. You are never supposed to join a negative club. If the club members are not adding sunshine and happiness to your life than please, don't join. You know the saying, "misery, loves company"... indeed it does, it's like taboo.

If you are struggling in life and you can't seem to keep up with the Joneses, well ... don't!

You don't have to keep up with anyone but yourself. You have an obligation to your immediate family and no one else.

If you have to cut the cable off or buy cheaper products because money is tight … don't take that personal. That's life and what we must do to be good stewards of our money. You cannot worry about what other people think ... what you must do is to live your life the best you can within your means and be happy. Your life is exactly that … your life and no one else's!

"I create my happiness everywhere I am! I am the controller of my happiness!" You should write that down and repeat that daily. Put it on your mirror in your bathroom or your car, wherever you will be able to read it out loud and remember it in your daily realm.

Repeat after me, *"I am the controller of my happiness!"* and mean it! Every day you open your eyes, you are the controller of how your day goes down. Anything can come into your world good or bad, but it's up to you to create the right outcome by your words, actions and reactions. There is a focus on how you act, but for some people, they become instinct.

You can smile instead of frown, you can laugh instead of smirking your lips, or you can simply be silent with a smile on your face … fake or not, sometimes you have to just act it out to create a happy environment for others.

I don't always want to smile but I do so that others will feel welcomed or loved. Often times if I fake it first, the real smiles come quickly for I am always reminded that my life is not always for myself but others as well and the gift of a smile is to be shared and not squandered!

Life, as you know it, can make you or break you. It doesn't matter who you are or what you have, if you are not careful you can end up in the lost and found, never to be claimed. I don't know about you, but I don't want to be unclaimed in anyone's lost and found. I want to be able to see the area for enhancement and do so accordingly.

If we keep ourselves lost we may not be able to find ourselves again in life and how sad would that be? When people can steal your joy, you feel less of a person and often create the person that they sadly molded you to be. You end up a sad and pathetic individual.

No one has the right to steal your joy unless you allow them to, kind of like giving them the key to your home and your safe deposit box.

No one has a right to say anything about your life unless you are breaking the law of some sort. Don't take it personally that others will be offended that you don't gossip and that you are trying to live a happy life.

They will try to tear you down instead of lift you up, but only you have the control to say otherwise. You don't have to even share your life with those in your circle unless they have a vested interest and it's a necessity as well as an asset.

You have to keep an evaluation on everyone, and everything in your life for if we allow any and everything to go on we will in no time creates the kind of life that is falling off and apart around us. The goal here is to enhance your life and not to destroy it.

One must always have a conscious mind of right and wrong but to truly give in to the finger pointing will be to give in to the devil. No one should be able to say anything bad that is true and worth talking about. Your life, full of sunshine and happiness should be lived in a way that doesn't give a second ear to any negative gossip about you. If it's out there like that, then we surely know it's not true so let's keep it moving.

If I can be allowed to be blunt as I usually am … excusing my French, you know I'm French right? Well … Who gives a crap what other people say or think about me? Not me, that's who and I sure am tired of people turning the other cheek when all I do is say hello and try to share the sunshine!

When people see me coming with my sun rays beaming and my smile shining bright ... they pull out their sunblock! Just like it was a disease.

People are so allergic to sunshine it's not funny. It's like an epidemic, like a plaque or something. You smile and greet people, and they look at you like you have said the rudest of words to them! I'm thinking, "Wow! Are you serious?"

I mean, can a friendly hello simply mean a friendly hello …. The point here is that the other person is now guilty of not being kind if they don't respond so how dare you to put them in that position and on they go with no guilt inside about a frown instead of a smile.

Look how long that took to go over when all they had to do was smile in the first place, and we wouldn't have to be writing this book.

Pay close attention. See the difference in the reaction of others when you have enhanced your peace of mind and changed the way you view things.

You are now upgraded remember, and therefore you are shining like a diamond. People will be watching you at all times, waiting for you to fall or falter off and go back to the old you. People will act happy that you are a new but will always have slight envy because they want the shine too.

Unfortunately, they have to find their sunshine and should not be allowed to steal yours. Watch how when you become happy and full of sunshine, that they pull out their sunblock so you cannot share that sunshine with them! They totally block it! *Lol!* Well, I would be, "Hey! Why would you want to block my happiness and sunshine?"

Please don't take it personally that people will not want to see you shine, will not want you to teach them how to shine and definitely do not want you getting glory for shinning. So watch out! For the manufacturer of sunblock has an unlimited supply. *Lol!* Please don't take it personally and keep shinning anyway!

Remembering to ...

- Don't take "others" personal

- Learn to not "react" but to "evaluate."

- Not to go back to your old ways

- Invite yourself to places

- Call people you love and admire

- Don't expect from others

- See the blessing in all things

- Everything is a learning experience

- Let sorry people be sorry people, all by themselves

- SMILE, always!

NOTES:

14 Loving You First

We know how to love from the moment we are born and well into our journey of life, but we often are not taught or simply neglect ourselves when it comes to love. We know how to love other people, but when it comes to our being, we fail miserably. When was the last time you scheduled yourself on your calendar and when was the last time you kept yourself on your calendar?

Like myself, probably a long time ... It's how we operate and how we learned to love. We were taught how to take care of the whole world but no one ever really taught us how to love ourselves first. Loving ourselves first is essential to life for if we do not know how to love ourselves, how well will we love others even though it's our best intention.

It's something to think about for everyone believes they know how to love and to receive it but in reality, we do not. I don't know about you, but I want to learn how to love myself and take continued courses throughout my life so that I can grow and prosper without losing myself again.

Learning to love YOU first ... That's HUGE!

Often in life, we are consumed with work, marriage, family, friends, and the demand for us can sometimes wear us out or keep us from doing us. That's ok, but you should not allow that to consume your whole world. You have to love yourself first so that everyone else falls into place.

Take yourself out to dinner, to a movie, get your nails done, go to the bookstore or simply take a hot bubble bath. Do something that is taking care of and loving you, whether you are a male or female.

Call my friend Demetrius and take yourself on a test drive of a luxury car of your choice if you live in California (You can find this info in the back of the book.) You have to speak what you want or need into your existence. It doesn't matter if you only have Toyota money ....test drive a Mercedes or Rolls Royce anyway! You never know what can happen. If you can dream it, you can be it or achieve it!

There has to be an agreement with yourself that you come first. If your mind is not right, your life will not be right, and the people that are in your circle will be affected as well. There may not be anyone to take care of you and or pamper you, but you can make your day how you need it to be, taking the time to understand your needs, as well as those in your care.

We only have control of us, and we need to remember that love comes when we create it, not when someone gives it to us. I had to learn how to love my children and then myself. I come from a family of strong women who held an ice type of relationship with people. Protecting the heart and the mind while dealing with the world is how I grew up and now that I am old enough to know better, I want to do better.

Loving me first is something that a lot of people in my circle cannot understand. Some people don't understand the fact that now that I love myself; I don't want to share a lot of things. I want to keep some things to myself because, in my life, I have shared everything forever. I love myself enough to have boundaries and limitations as to how much of my life I will lease out to others.

If you pull out your view master slide, you can see that in our past life we gave over and beyond our call of duty to other people, yet always neglecting ourselves. But right now at this moment, you must commit to love you and only you before you can love anyone, and I mean anyone else.

What are the rules for love? Where do you learn to love yourself? It's not as easy as it sounds I know but rest assure you can learn anything you want to learn in due time. You first need to understand what it actually means and you first must want to learn it.

You know the saying, you can lead a horse to water, but you surely cannot make him drink it. There are so many things in life that we wanted yet never went for it. Sometimes we see the big picture and do nothing to make it a reality. We dream big gigantic dreams and dream often, but who teaches us how to achieve it? Well, did you realize that all things in life are not meant to be done alone? There are people put in our circles for those specific reasons, to help us through the journey of life.

When I pull out my view master, I can see that there is an opportunity for me to learn to love myself as well as others. I first have to prepare my mind. Once I get my mind right, anything is possible.

Taking me out for lunch and to a movie is a great way to start my weekend or my day off. I love taking myself out. It's so much fun... I can go alone or with a friend or colleague but I make sure there is no business involved, strictly fun and happiness.

On occasion, I go hang out at the bookstore. There are so many great books out there to read and learn new things about life. It's free to do, and you may even come home with something that you just couldn't resist. Life is going to be what we make it and the moment you learn to love yourself first is the day you will know that you are alive. Yes, alive ...

Oh, sure you are living, but are you alive? Well, what that means is that we are born into a life that we have no control over, and we are expected to get an A+ on a test without being able to study for it ahead of time. It's like sitting someone down to take a test without even knowing what the test consists of. Just here, figure this out, and you better do well at it. Ok ... what?

That's not how life is supposed to be lived. We are supposed to be taught a curriculum of life skills before we are released to the world.

How not nice to release people into a world they know nothing about because they didn't have to know anything about it. Remember, we are talking about young adults who are always being told by their parents that they have no control over anything... it's none of their business, its grown folks business, etc. Remember that? (*laughing*) Oh yes, you do! Well,...they don't know how to live life or how to love. For some people, it may come natural, and for others, it may not come at all, and you may need to be taught how. If you don't come from a loving family, then the odds of you knowing how to love are slim, especially knowing how to love yourself. But it's no problem; you can learn anything you desire. If the desire exists, the opportunity exists!

Loving YOU will come easy with time. Everything takes time to implement, be patient with YOU and take one day at a time. You can only live for today, for this moment, so don't be so hard on yourself when it comes to learning or reinventing your life. Everyone has to be taught; it's a matter of who you are willing to learn from. You don't have to use everything you learn as it is given but learn how to take what you learn and create your own version, add your own ingredient to the recipe.

Loving yourself can be done by acknowledging that you deserve to be loved. Look at your view master and see the love that waits for you every day. It is not your past, nor your future; it's your today. You can only live for today, the past is gone and tomorrow is not guaranteed. Today, I love me, and because I first love me, I can now love you as well.

Today …

I learned how to touch my heart with my hand … leaving it there, palm down, skin to skin, letting my heart know that it is loved and appreciated. I have to be the one that lets my body and my mind know that I am loved. There can surely be more love added to the table at any time from others, but the most important love you experience should be coming from you!

Teach it to your children and your grandchildren. Teach them to love themselves first… as they grow, they will be remarkable people because of it. Sharing love that they have created and nurtured for years before onto the world would simply make the world a better place.
Ok, so I can dream …. I believe in fairytales!

Touch your heart, your kidney, and your different body parts in alternation if you like, as long as you let your important body parts know they are loved and appreciated, massage them a little. Once you have accomplished learning to love yourself, you will have great joy in sharing that with others … wait and see.

I am so happy to have the revelation of finding myself in life. I am so excited to implement new things and re-create some things here and there. I don't have anything drastic to change, but I will admit that what I want to change is my attitude about people. I love people and want to help change the world for the better, but it's very challenging to find good in what I perceive to be an evil world.

Learning to accept the fact that everyone is not like myself so I cannot expect "what I would do" in my everyday life. I have to learn to adapt to each situation as it is presented without blocking the goodness that could come of it being afraid of letting my guards down only to be disappointed …. again!

We can break any cycle that we want to break as long as we get our mind right first. Loving ourselves means not allowing negative things to come into our lives. Loving myself means to know when it's time to allow the love of others in or when it's time to remove it. Remember, loving others as well as loving yourself is not easy. It may be the hardest thing in life you will do, maintaining love.

Loving the person you are today is your goal. Make it your life goal. Loving you for who you are, not for what you have, but for who you know you can be and what you are willing to do to achieve it. One step at a time, one day at a time is all you can do.

Breaking the cycle ...

Breaking the cycle of life or family (learned behavior) is something each of us must remember is always a part of our journey. We are taught things from other people's perspective and often that does not fit our life ... It was the person that taught it to you or the person that taught it to them... You see, even though the concept is the same, the design is supposed to, by birthright, be different. Learn to learn with alterations. Take what you learn and redesign it for your life.

You will discover there are lots of things you knew already; this was just an enhancement of life. It's perfectly normal to learn, redesign, teach, learn more, redesign, and teach more. See how the pattern is always to learn something first, after you learn it, redesign it or not, after you redesign it, it's now ready to be taught to someone else ... the more you learn, the more you can teach. Sharing the gifts of life is how it's meant to be, how the world was created. To not be selfish and openly teach other individuals something that can help their life is a gift and not to use those gifts are just a waste of human space.

If you want to learn something, you have to ask someone to teach it to you if in fact, you are unable to learn by observance. You can either pick up the phone book (I'm old school lol try the internet) and find someone in that profession or ask a friend, church member or colleague for a referral of someone in that profession. Asking friends and family is always a good thing; just remember to do your research before accepting other opinions. Just because they have a great testimony about it doesn't mean they are right for you and or your need. Take the info and research.

Learning to love you is the greatest accomplishment one will ever do in life. By all means, go all the way but without hurting others around you. Sometimes it may be unnecessary to do or not do something just because you love yourself ... Keep the feelings and reception of others in mind at all times. Sometimes we have to do things we would prefer not to do to keep the love going around.

How do I love myself? By changing your hairstyle to something you absolutely love, not just something you like or something you can deal with, but something that makes you feel sexy and fun call my friend Leroy at Supercuts, he'll hook you up (no matter where you are). Or, by changing the style shirts that you buy so that you feel like a million bucks! You can do that as inexpensively as possible, just find a way to enhance your wardrobe so that you are different and feel more loved. And remember, we are not looking for the approval from others, we are doing what makes us happy, what makes us feel loved and appreciated for ourselves.

So...get, a haircut, change your wardrobe and buy a new pair of shoes that totally fits you. Step outside of your box, or better yet...get rid of the box altogether!

Do things that make you smile and make you have living orgasms. I live my life in such a way that at any moment, anywhere, I may have a living orgasm. What's a living orgasm you may ask? It's that moment when something jumps into your heart and your soul so deep it makes you scream out loud from your inner being. It's like the living orgasm you get when you see your winning lotto numbers or when you have the sexual orgasm of your life. Either way, you look at it, its excitement from your soul.

I love walking in the rain without worrying about my hair or shoes. I love going to the park and having picnics. I love being at a local baseball game, professional or not it doesn't matter to me, as long as I'm at the game… fun is what I'm looking for. The local baseball team here has a great crowd, The Stockton Ports, you know… it's going to be what I make it, and if I make it fun than fun, it shall be.

It doesn't always have to cost you money to do it either; you can do things that are free like going to the bookstore and just hanging out or going to the park or take a walk on the walking trails where you will see and meet lots of people. I love going to the local baseball games either alone or with a group of friends … I have fun either way. The ballpark is beautiful, and the sun is always out just right, it's just a great atmosphere to be in, and the team is great. When I go with friends, we eat lots, drink more and just have a great time. One day you should come on out and have some fun of your own … any event at any time, get season tickets to The Stockton Ports!

Many things in life will cost you some dollars and cents but just try to be more creative and keep those expenses down if you need to. If you don't need to, enjoy your new seat at the ballpark.

We don't want to create bigger problems than we already have. Be mindful of your need to love yourself. You will not always need to buy expensive clothing; sometimes you're overrating your "I deserve this" or "I work hard" to get what you want and not what you need. Just be mindful. Loving you can be done right there in the comfort of your own home. Take a hot bath instead of a shower. A hot bath is like an apple a day; it will defiantly keep the doctor away. Even if your bath is short and sweet, take a hot bath instead of a shower a few times a week. It gets the blood flowing through your body as well as your mind; it changes that pep in your step, just a little bit.

You can buy a new bathrobe, one that makes you feel manly or pretty. Things in your immediate environment make you act how it makes you feel so if it doesn't make you feel anything at all, well how do you think you are looking to the world.

I want to walk into my home and feel love. I want to see love on my walls (photos of flowers, family and friends), I want to feel the love of us talking around the kitchen table or sitting by the fire watching a movie together. We can barbeque in the backyard for dinner and have a picnic right there on the lawn. There are so many different ways to learn to love; you can make a list if you like and start there.

Whatever you choose to do is supposed to make you happy, make you smile. From the moment you open your eyes in the morning is a new opportunity to do and be, anything you want to do or be. We have a choice as to how we live our life, good or bad. We have a choice in our attitude and our acceptance of others. We have choices. The choices we make are a whole different ball game, at a different stadium.

Learning to talk things out, writing things down and reading them out loud will help you in all aspects of life regardless of the situation. Learning to sit first, listen, write it down, analyze it, discuss it out loud, agree to remain mindful and proceed as you need to. Learn to create a process that will help you have positive outcomes even if it's not what you want. At least if you learn to have a process, you will help your mind to be right. Keeping your mind right is very important. If your mind is not right, your world will crumble.

Why are we constantly beating ourselves up over our past mistakes? Why are we constantly beating everyone else up for their past mistakes? It's a normal brain game that we play every day.

Learning to love ourselves will help us to not fester anger, resentment or unforgiveness. Releasing your mind to such things will help you live a more prosperous and happy life. The past is now a part of yesterday. If you don't release today, how can you prepare to receive your tomorrow? You will not be able to receive it fairly, let me tell you. Learn to release all things that have already taken place, all things that can no longer be changed, all things that were unnecessary and all things that have no follow-ups or extensions. It's now time to stand tall, pull back your shoulders, and show your smile on your face as if you just won a gold medal and posing for a photo on the wheat box.

Loving you will become a part of your DNA if you allow it. Once you get the habit of taking care of you first, it will become a necessity that you will not allow to be broken... for no one. Have fun loving you for you! For if you don't do it...who will?

Sometimes the expectation of others gets the best of us. Often we expect others to want to love us and make us happy. That is most certainly the wrong attitude to take when it comes to our own life. We are to be loved as a child, as every child should be shown love and taught how to love as well. We teach our children, family, and friends how to love us by the way we treat ourselves. If you want to know how you are thought of, then look in your view master at how each person in your life treats you and why they treat you that way.

It most often is the way you have treated yourself in front of them as well as what you allowed them to do as a response to that action. It happens over time ... you live how you live, right or wrong, that's not the issue, but what you do is what people see. People, in turn, will, in their mind form an opinion about you based on how you act around them or in their circle. Their reactions to you are then created in your mind, and now you have your vision not even realizing the relationship you have with people are how you first relation with yourself.

Remembering to ...

- Tell and show your body that you love it.

- Have a barbeque dinner or a picnic in the backyard.

- Go to a drive-in movie.

- Find a new hairstyle that is sexy and fun.

- Skip work and hang out at the waterfront with good food and maybe a friend.

- Buy a new pair of shoes or shirt.

- Go to the bookstore and read one new book every two weeks.

- Learn a new trade or hobby.

- Get a manicure and/or pedicure.

- Go to the park or church.

NOTES:

15 Stepping Into A New Beginning

Stepping out of Purgatory Living is now a part of your new DNA, and you should be proud to repeat, that you will never lose yourself again. The whole world has been looking for you, and you have been blessed enough to be able to remove yourself from the lost and found, most wanted list, prayer lists, critical list, milk cartons and post office signs ... you have been officially found alive and well! No longer in Purgatory Living! Congratulations on being found, I am very proud of you!

It takes a lot of work to be found in life, and you should be very proud of your success to do so. Not everyone comes out of it alive and well. Often in life, we stay stuck in misery and heartache, long work hours and no happy hours. We make life complex simply by working for the rent and mortgage, and there is nothing else left of us to share with the world.

That's how we end up in the purgatory of living, staying lost in life by not living in our today. Well, today you can be found if you are not found already. Today can be the first day of the rest of your life or the last day of your life... it's always your choice, as you desire.

Stepping into a new beginning is a great joy that must be celebrated. If you stepped out with family or friends, celebrate together, if you did it all alone, well get a group together and share with them your experience and thank them for their patience through your new transition.

Learning who you are is a great accomplishment...upgrading your life and or your business took a lot of work but you can, or you did do it. It's always going to be up to you.

Once you learn a new way to live your life, you should always have an upgrade... You know, as they do for cars, cell phones or computers. You upgrade your phone regularly most likely as well as your car, why not upgrade you, aren't you worth more of the investment than useless things? Upgrade your life regularly so that you never become outdated. You must keep up to your present day to your present time and that time is today and today only. Remember, yesterday has already passed and tomorrow is not guaranteed.

I didn't find you, you found yourself. You knew where you were the whole time. You just didn't want to bother with coming out of hiding and stepping out. There are so many things in life that we just don't want to deal with, but the truth of the matter is that we must deal with it, and we must deal with it TODAY!

Preparing for all of your transitions should be a part of your list of life: Birthday, Anniversary, New Baby, College, Marriage, Becoming a Senior or Death.

Have you pre-prepared for all of your transitions in life? Have you saved the money that will be needed to live-out all of your transitions? Have you prepared for your death?

Having a prepared life is essential to being happy. Rest assured, life will move on with or without you. The more prepared you are, the happier, and at peace, you will be. And when that happens, the whole world changes and life is good!

You found yourself right in the nick of time... but then again, you weren't even lost, just going through transitions…life is too short to be lost in Purgatory. Life is too short to lose, so much time is wasted talent. We have an obligation to ourselves and our family to know who we are and to act accordingly. How do you ensure that you are never lost again? Well while life is never a guarantee for we have to rely on so many people that are of this world, that we just have to make sure to do our part, to take initiatives and find healthy alternatives, to live life to the fullest, to care about ourselves and others to be a part of change and to always make a difference. We should be quick to lend a helping hand, to live for others within our means. To give to life what we want life to give —TO LIVE!

Never allow it to be the END.

HAPPY AND FREE! You are ordained to BE by me, Summer B!

Remembering to ...

- **JUST BE HAPPY!**

"Happiness will always be what you create it to be. From the moment you open your eyes each new day; you have a choice to be happy and free! Use your choices wisely!" —Summer B

NOTES:

HEALING YOUR MIND BODY AND SOUL
WITH DR. JEANETTE (Jet) REED (Denver, Colorado)

What is healing ...

I have been studying the human body and healing methods since I was a 16-year-old girl who managed to get a job at a health food store. I knew nothing about nutrition or vitamins. Vegetables were served as an unrecognizable spoonful of mush. We were well fed in my family; it's just that this was the result of a haggard mother cooking for six other people. I am sure at one point in the evening those zucchinis were crisp and just right for the tasting. By the time she rounded up five girls, dad put the begging dog out, well, the vegetables didn't have a chance.

As I began my studies and started cooking for myself, I fell in love with fresh food. I had never tasted a leek or endive. Fresh carrot and apple juices were served at my local health food store, and I loved it! I started to feel more alive, had more energy and my acne cleared up. I was a believer. I began using herbs to detoxify my liver to help with my acne. I learned that my chronic constipation was toxic to my body, which I needed to move that garbage out. I began using multiple vitamins and could feel the difference. Even a simple B complex vitamin daily would make things better.

Over the next 36 years, I would learn a vast amount of information regarding healing. I studied herbology, nutrition, aromatherapy, midwifery, massage, naturopathy, jin shin, acupressure, Ayurvedic sciences, reiki and finally chiropractic care.

I received my Doctor of Chiropractic in 1996 from Life West Chiropractic College. I had the honor of studying with the founder of Network Spinal Analysis, Dr. Donald Epstein. Studying with him blew the socks off my limited understanding about healing, and he opened up many doors, asked many provocative questions which moved the box around my limited thinking. I felt a deeper understanding of why the current paradigm that most health care operates within was not health care. I started to question, 'What is healing?' and after all these years I have come to this conclusion.

Healing is an inside job. When we cut our finger on the potato peeler and end up with a Band-Aid, we have a sore finger. But do we lose sleep at night worrying about whether or not our cut is going to heal? Do we wonder if the cut will close?

Will the scab form properly? Will the skin heal so well that eventually the scar will be so small we won't be able to find it? No, we do not. We know, from experience, that the cut will heal. We have seen it happen time and time again. The body's defense system sent in the coagulants blood cells to stop the bleeding. Then it sends in the white blood cells to protect against infection. Then comes the collagen and the tissue repair army which creates the scab, replaces cells with different tissue-skin cells. One day the skin is so repaired that the scab falls off and we see fresh, new skin on our finger. It is truly a miracle.

The power that made the body heals the body. It happens no other way. The innate intelligence, inborn, governs every little chemical reaction in our bodies. 2000 chemical reactions are happening in your body every second. And the body is doing all of this while we sit and drink our cup of tea. We are thinking about the next project, but our body's intelligence is organizing, controlling and regulating the 70 trillion cells in our body. That is a magnificent job. It's an inside job.

Healing can be uncomfortable, "Dang, that scab can itch." Healing can be inconvenient, "Dang, that burns when the lemon juice touches my cut."
Healing can look like throwing up when we have eaten something our body deems as poisonous. It is healthy to throw up; the toxins are released. It can be healthy to have diarrhea for the same reason; toxins are leaving the body. Healing can look like a fever, the body's natural way to raise the temperature so the bacteria will be killed.

Healing can be emotional- crying is a release, laughing brings strong peptides to our system. Bruce Lipton in his groundbreaking book, "Molecules of Emotion" showed us that thoughts change the protein structure of the cell membrane. Therefore, the brain of the cell, the membrane, is changed by a human thought and this changes what the cell allows in and out. The thought pattern altered the health of that red blood cell.

The current model of healing we all grew up in is not a healing model at all. It is a disease and sickness care model. A healing model would include nutrition, colon health, water intake, exercise, and many other modalities which increase the body's immune system and alignments, such as chiropractic care and acupuncture. When my father was dying from complications of his chronic lymphocytic leukemia, not one doctor ever asked us, "Jack, what are you eating?

How are your bowel movements? Are you drinking enough water?" Not one.

The only offerings were a prescription and then more prescriptions for the undesirable effects of the first prescription, sometimes called "side effects" but they are undesirable effects. Big pharmaceuticals want us to believe that side effects are a rare thing, but they are not. They just aren't the effect wanted to stop the symptom. And just because the symptom stops, this doesn't mean the patient is healed. True healing looks for the cause of the symptom. Why is the body producing too much stomach acid which has created the ulcer?

How can we reduce the stress level of this patient and change their diet so that the body doesn't produce the extra acid? These are the healing questions to ask. Ulcers are not caused by a lack of Prilosec in the bloodstream.

As a chiropractor, I would also analyze the middle back area for a misaligned bone; we call this a subluxation. This middle back area houses the nerves which control the digestive system, and if the bone is subluxated, the nerve which controls the stomach may have a reduced flow of information or an increased flow. Both alterations may affect the digestion of the patient.

I would adjust the bones back to their normal alignment, thereby bringing balance to the nervous system. My patient would let me know if their symptoms decreased or ceased. I would continue to adjust this area if the alignment wasn't correct, regardless of the symptom changing. This surprises people because we are all taught, if the symptom is gone, we are fixed. Well, it's not true.

Gagging our health by the presence of symptoms or not is not an accurate way to gauge health. A woman with a tumor in her breast often has no pain, yet the cancer is growing. For women my age, a common cause of death is a sudden cardiac arrest, in which the woman never felt any chest or heart pain. And she is dead. Here is a synopsis of a handout I give all new patients which describe the difference between what our current medical system is attempting, curing a symptom or an illness and healing, which is the antithesis of curing.

Curing is done to you, it happens from the outside in, it is passive, it treats the symptom, it singles out one part of you, it is quick but short-lived, it restores you to where you were before, and it focuses on the ailment. You do healing, it happens from the inside out, it is active, it addresses the cause, it encompasses all of you, it is gradual yet lasting, it leaves you better than you were before and it focuses on you.

One little step at a time, perhaps increasing your vegetable intake and reducing your sugar- this is a self-generated healing action to take. It is empowering to heal, a person takes personal responsibility for their health and creates change based on a desire to having better health.

U.S. prescription drug spending dropped in 2012 to $325.8 billion to the 2011 figure of $329.2. That is a good sign. Our country accounts for 34 percent of the world market for pharmaceuticals. That is not a good sign. The World Health Organization in 2000 ranked U.S.A. 38th, under Costa Rica and above Slovenia. France was #1 and Italy #2.

Do you see a problem with these facts? Our country spends 325 plus billion dollars on pharmaceuticals, yet we are rated ridiculously low. It is a valuable conversation to be having with each other, with our families and our friends. "Why is this so and what can we do about it?" Asking that question is the first step on a journey which will empower us; it will harness the creative energy of the group and find real solutions to our health crisis. And that is healing in the making.

—by Dr. Jeanette Reed
www.drjetreed.com

Health and Wellness with ...

Dr. Robert K. Walker Ph.D.

Dr. Robert K. Walker Ph.D. is a health ambassador for a Health & Wellness company entitled Youngevity International with its Headquarters being located in Chula Vista, California and Youngevity owns a Plant Mineral Mine in Salt Lake City, Utah where our organic minerals are cultivated from a multi-million-year-old mineral mine which has 77 plant minerals embedded in the soil, that is 3,000 feet below sea level.

Over the past 20 years my company Youngevity has promoted and repaired over 350 million patient's health challenges such as Asthma, ADD/ADHD, Breast Cancer, Diabetes, Eczema, Glaucoma, Heart Disease, Infertility and Kidney Failure because 2-Time Nobel Prize Winner Dr. Linus Paulin's research shows that "every disease and every ailment in the body is caused by a mineral deficiency of the 90 Essential Nutrients. Because every cell in your body regenerates every 90 days, and they need 5 components to preserve your health, and they are: 60 minerals, 16 vitamins, 12 amino acids, 2 essential fatty acids and antioxidants which will supply the body with the proper nutrients that will fight off the 900 diseases that will attack the body.

So every nutrient has at least 10 diseases connected to them because of a mineral deficiency according to the 2-Time Nobel Peace Prize Winner Dr. Linus Paulin, whose research shows that every ailment and every disease is caused by a mineral deficiency and according to the U. S. Senate Document 264 which says that "since 1936, the soil of the Earth is depleted of the minerals where food is grown that we need to sustain perfect health.

And the U.S.D.A. says that "95% of all Americans are mineral deficient because over the past 100 years our soils have decreased by 85% and because we also consume Genetically Modified foods (GMO's), we also are not getting the proper nutrition in our diet. So with these GMO's and processed foods that we are consuming, we are not going to see certain illnesses dissipate from our bodies because we are stressing ourselves to the limit.

So again the Endocrine system is a closed circuit, and if the Pancreas is stressed, then you stress out the Spleen and if the Spleen is stressed,

then you stress out the Liver and if the Liver is stressed,

then you stress out the Gall Bladder and if the Gall Bladder is stressed,

then you stress out the Kidneys and if the Kidneys is stressed,

then you stress out the Heart and if the Heart is stressed,

then you stress out the Lungs and if the Lungs is stressed,

your respiratory breathing is affected, and you will need life support.

Every 90 days every cell in your body regenerates and needs five components to sustain perfect health: Minerals, Vitamins, Amino Acids, EFA's and Antioxidants. The process foods that we consume contain unhealthy chemicals, processed sugars, processed deli meats, margarine (trans-fat), sugary cereals, fast-foods, microwave popcorn, pop-tarts, blended coffee drinks and sodas (regular & diet) which feeds cancer.

We have determined that 80% of diseases are falling into 4 Categories:

Blood Sugar Imbalance

Calcium Deficiency

Digestive Disorder

and EFA/Cholesterol which can fight off the 900 diseases in your body.

In a study done in 2009, according to the CDC which says that "every year 15 million patients are killed, infected and injured by the medical doctor with his/her diagnostic treatments and unnecessary surgeries".

Also the U.S. National Poison Data System says that "no one has ever died from taking over-the-counter minerals, vitamins and herbs but only 600 adverse reactions from an overdose and 100,000 patients died from properly prescribed over-the-counter drugs called non-steroidal anti-inflammatory (NSAID's) so what happen to the medical Hippocratic Oath that says "Do No Harm" to your patients.

The body needs 90 essential nutrients aka plant minerals and vitamins in order to sustain perfect health every day, so if you want an **FREE health consultation** just call my office at **888-383-0929** or email **robertkwalker1@gmail.com** then after you get your remedy protocol you can go to our website … **www.drrobertkwalker.youngevity.com** where you can get the proper organic minerals and vitamins to repair and promote perfect health in your body.

The CONSULTATION is FREE if you make the call or email!

Thinking of you ... I say THANK YOU!

To Bill T. for the encouragement to stick with the reality of this book and not allowing me to sugar coat its title. Dr. Jeanette (Jet) Reed and Sandy L., for being my angels and helping me come through my purgatory living. And to my grandchildren, Mariah, Elijah, King Joseph, Vanessa, Anthony & Andrew for being my new inspiration to living, you brighten my every day.

I would especially like to thank the women in my social media group ... THE MIND OF EVERY WOMAN EXPOSED! I thank you for your willingness to open your hearts to be exposed through learning, sharing, healing and growing, all 333 members, you are an inspiration to others, and you are an inspiration to yourself...always BELIEVE.

Ms. Kat for sharing the love, and encouragement through purgatory 2 (lol). But most importantly, to Ms. Amelia (Emily @Olivas Chiropractic, Stockton, Ca) for making me BUCK up every day along the way, I am so grateful!

Loving you all UNCONDITIONALLY!

~Summer B.

FRIENDS OF SUMMER BRADSHAU ...
That has started their own business and or set out to make a difference! No affiliations just inspiration and motivation! If they can do it, so can you, feel free to ask them how or just check them out and see their adventure and progress.

Dr. Jeanette "Jet" Reed,
Subluxation Chiropractic Specialist
Network Spinal Analysis
 www.drjetreed.com
www.bemeramerica.com/jet

Tamika Harris - Fashion Consultant & Speaker
UBER Driver Code - m1x5ejekue   Join The Team
Legal Shield
 www.tamikasharris.legalshieldassociate.com

Mario Sanchez Art Work often featured with Betti Ono Gallery
(skull and hammer man)

Anyka Barber, Owner - Support your local art gallery
Betti Ono Gallery, 1427 Broadway
Oakland, CA 94612
www.bettiono.com
www.facebook.com/bettiono

Greedy Geez (music writing)
http://www.datpiff.com/GREEDY-GEEZ-The-Lack-Of-Love-2-
mixtape.788638.html
https://www.youtube.com/user/GEEZOFGASSNATION/videos
GREEDY GEEZ x HOT BOI JUICE - HEAVEN OR HELL
https://youtu.be/_WVT_7wBH5Q

Leroy Thomas "The Hair Master"
Founder and Owner of:
Salon Manaz -12513 San Pablo Ave. Richmond, CA
www.facebook.com/Leroy.Salon.Manaz
Supercuts/Mastercuts -Regis brand SF Bay Area
Honolulu Hawaii-Kauai Hawaii
 Senior District Leader

MORE FRIENDS OF Summer b

Rosemary Hazen, Book Editor
Educational Consultant
Usborne Books and More!
UsborneP3571@gmail.com
www.myUBAM.com/P3571
www.facebook.com/reading4kids

Sharon Carrell, Certified Massage Therapist
Doterra Essential Oils
1341 Robinhood Dr., Stockton, CA 95207
(209) 329-1121

Demetrius Walls, BMW MERCEDES
Email: demetrius.walls@facebook.com
 www.facebook.com/demetrius.walls

Don Marine Boating Company
#64 Brickfield Village, Waterloo Rd.,
Carapichaima, Chaguanas, Trinidad, and Tobago
donmarineboats@hotmail.com
www.facebook.com/DonMarineBoatingCompany

Jazzy Jewels By Tiffany
Custom orders
www.facebook.com/jazzyjewels30

Dwayne Mack
DMack Best Dress Threads
http://www.dmackbdt.com
His clothing designs and innovations will allow you to step
up your wardrobe and become one of the best dressed.

More Please! Cookies and Brownies
https://www.facebook.com/Morepleasecookies
"Treat Yourself" baked by Cheyenne Wright

Docs Q'in Pit Stop —THE BEST BAR-B-Q IN THE VALLEY!!
421 Maze Blvd., Modesto, CA 95351
www.docsqnpit.com

Angelina Perkins
Shop Pinkalina
shoppinkalina@gmail.com
www.shop.com/ShopPinkalina

Tony Bear, Radio DJ
www.Tonybear.com

William Belcher
Pyramid Media
Stick and Move (up and coming movie)
http://www.pyramidmediavision.com
willbelcherproductions@yahoo.com

Kelly Mayes, 5 Linx JOIN the team
email: boutitbiz01@yahoo.com
www.facebook.com/MTGjewels

Hand & Hand Foundation (Non-Profit Organization)
In conjunction with local and national charities working to build our
children productive citizens by affording them with the opportunities every
American child should have food, shelter, protection, and education.

Hand & Hand Foundation is a Children's & Environmental charity, we work to help provide
what's needed for our children while working to protect our planet's resources. We only have two
futures, our children, and our environment, without either we cease to exist.
www.handandhandfoundation.org
www.facebook.com/Hand-Hand-Foundation-195267505708
https://twitter.com/HHFCEO

Bernadette Anderson - Juice Plus, Next best thing to fruits and Vegetables

www.wholesomewarrior.juice plus.com
www.wholesomewarrior.com

MADHAV K., Designer
Purgatory Living Book Cover design by Madhav K.
Photo credit: Madhav K.
www.fiverr.com/madhavkmcy

#OneOFMyUpgrades

My current chiropractor who specializes in subluxation is essential to my life. He treats my whole body and not just my back. He is also a Network Spinal Analysis specialist. I've done the research, I have experienced the treatment and can testify that everyone needs to be educated in chiropractic care. My physicians could not help fix my issues; they only medicated me. With this treatment, I can function much better and on my own accord.

I cannot live my life without chiropractic care, and I'm thankful I was smart enough to do the research and follow through with a treatment plan. Thanks to chiro care I can live a happier and healthier life. And so can you. If you are not in the area, find someone close to you. It's essential to good health (if you qualify). And a long Gevity future. https://wiseworldseminars.com/network-spinal-analysis

Some Benefits Of Chiro Care: *(I have not used my asthma medication for almost five years now thanks to the care I received from Network Spinal Analysis care.)*

From Infants, children, adults to seniors …everyone benefits from chiro care!

In Infants & children: Asthma. ADHD . EarAches . BedWetting . Respiratory Infections. Allergies . Scoliosis . BackPack Pain. Toddler Falls Birth Misalignments

In Adults: Asthma. Back Pain. Headaches . Migraines . Neck Pain. Bed Wetting. High Blood Pressure. Joint Pain. Diabetes . Healthy Pregnancy Fertility Male & Female. Boost Immune System. Arthritis . Scoliosis and more …

In Seniors: "All above" with the addition to Increased balance and coordination. Decreased Joint Degeneration. Decreased incidence of falling. Increase range of motion of the spine and extremities

Dr. Rick Bonar is a Stockton chiropractor who serves Stockton and the surrounding communities in CA.

Dr. Rick Bonar uses chiropractic care to improve the health and wellness in all areas of patient's lives, whether they are having problems with back pain or neck pain, or just want to start feeling better when they wake up in the morning. Dr. Bonar takes a "whole person" approach in chiropractic care, which means looking for the underlying causes of disease, discomfort, and pain, as opposed to just treating the symptoms. Many seemingly unrelated symptoms often arise from imbalances in the spinal column, and Dr. Bonar will be able to determine the root of the pain and create a personalized chiropractic and wellness plan to suit each patient's individual needs. Under the supervision and care of our caring and skilled chiropractor, patients report higher functioning in all areas of their lives. www.familychirostockton.com

Healthy living is essential to living. Treat yourself to better health.

HANDBAGS For HUMANITY

Handbags for Humanity is organized through Summer Bradshau @ The Bradshau Company, together with Hand & Hand Foundation. A mission of humanity to help homeless families and those with children, secure temporary - permanent housing through resource and referrals or monetary donations raised through our Handbags For Humanity project from individual or group donations of new or slightly used designer handbags, wallets and or briefcase and luggage.

Our mission is to help build stronger communities through education, training, resource, and referrals and resolving homeless outbreaks in all communities of people.

JOIN US in the fight against homelessness by donating or asking your community of family and friends to donate a new or gently used, designer handbags, wallets, briefcase or luggage, etc. NO money required. You have already spent it and it's most likely not being used to its full potential. Imagine it helping save the children from the cold.

The program will then auction or sale all donated items and use the proceed to help homeless families secure shelter and regain their ability to stability and peace.

HOST A "HANDBAG FOR HUMANITY" PARTY and ask your co-workers, family, and friends to donate their unused or barely used items to help make a difference in the lives of children. Help them to come home off the streets with self-respect and dignity!

You will be able to follow our progress through our variety of virtual portals where we will share with you regularly our progress within communities. Our mission and our reality will be provided for all to share and see as we are blessed with help worldwide and above. We need your help, and we are willing to meet you at the door and give you a key!

JOIN US ... HANDBAGS FOR HUMANITY! Everyone makes a difference and every family matters!

We also will help families that are in need of work clothing. Going back into the workforce is hard enough but especially hard if you don't have the proper clothing and the funding to purchase what you need. We will be helping people who need that small boost in life that will help them secure the simple basics that come easily to the majority. Un-used executive, name brand or not, suit, tie, dress shirt, and shoes are greatly needed in our pursuit of giving. If you have even just one piece to donate, you have blessed one person.

We thank you for your generosity and look forward to receiving your heartfelt donation soon. Time is always of the great essence for homeless families. Most have lost faith and may not know how to carry on, but with your donation, we can help give comfort to a child's family right when they need it most.

... giving back to our community of peoples! So why not join me and we can give to our communities together! You know ...as people. You are welcome to be a part our team, for together everyone accomplishes more.

You have a chance to choose to help someone in life. If we choose to work together, we can come up with some awesome solutions and not just temporary. All we need is a few helping hands that will surely become friends.

©https://www.facebook.com/handbagsforhumanity

#NoOneLeftBehind   #HandbagsForHumanity

The communication is free … utilize the wisdom, be blessed with the knowledge and love.

~Summer Bradshau - The Bradshau Company
Email: tbcinfo@att.net
www.facebook.com/BradshauCompany
www.summerbradshau.wordpress.com

https://www.facebook.com/Purgatoryliving

Purgatory Living: Stepping out of the Purgatory of living and stepping into a new beginning!
by Summer N. Bradshau et Amazon
Link: http://a.co/cJfoGOS

THANK YOU!

www.ingramcontent.com/pod-product-compliance
Lightning Source LLC
Chambersburg PA
CBHW052008090426

42741CB00008B/1608